URBAN POLICY AND HOUSING

D1434952

**Recent publications of
the South African Institute of Race Relations**

Claire Pickard-Cambridge, *Sharing the Cities: Residential desegregation
in Harare, Windhoek and Mafikeng* (1988)

John Dreijmanis, *The Role of the South African Government
in Tertiary Education* (1988)

Claire Pickard-Cambridge, *The Greying of Johannesburg* (1988)

Chris Heymans, *The Politics of Creation: An assessment of
government-created bodies for Africans in
South Africa* (1988)

Chris Heymans, *Akkommodasie sonder Demokrasie: Regeringsliggame
vir swart politieke verteenwoordiging in
Suid-Afrika* (1987)

Ben MacLennan, *Glenmore: The story of a forced removal (1987)*

Vanessa Gaydon, *Race against the Ratios: The why and the how of
desegregating teacher training* (1987)

Melville Festenstein and Claire Pickard-Cambridge, *Land and Race:
South Africa's Group Areas and Land Acts* (1987)

Charles Simkins, *Reconstructing South African Liberalism* (1986)

Charles Simkins, *Liberalism and the Problem of Power* (1986)

Alan Paton, *Federation or Desolation* (1985)

These are available from:

**The Publications Department,
South African Institute of Race Relations,
P O Box 31044,
2017 Braamfontein**

URBAN POLICY AND HOUSING

Case studies on negotiation in PWV townships

By

Paul Hendler

South African Institute of Race Relations
1988

Published by the South African Institute of Race Relations
Auden House, 68 De Korte Street,
Braamfontein, Johannesburg, 2001 South Africa
Copyright © South African Institute of Race Relations, 1988
PD 15/88
ISBN 0-86982-342-6 c T
ISSN 1011-5552

b 00377584l

Printed by Galvin & Sales, Cape Town

CONTENTS

INTRODUCTION

During the mid 1980s, violent conflict in the African townships around the major cities, accompanied by the appearance of street committees and alternative plans for education and township administration, prompted a belief that a new society was being shaped amidst the dusty streets of the townships. But, by 1987, the state's security forces had rolled back many of the advances made by its opponents. While they appeared to have reimposed township order, however, they had not succeeded in establishing the legitimacy of official black local authorities. Nor had political resistance in some townships ended: rent boycotts continued to frustrate the authorities. A stalemate between the government and anti-apartheid civic associations had developed which, to some commentators, could be ended only by negotiation.

This report attempts to explore possibilities for negotiation in the African townships of the Pretoria/Witwatersrand/Vereeniging (PWV) region. Because many of the conflicts of the past few years centred directly or indirectly around housing, it looks specifically at the prospects for negotiation around this issue by examining the attitudes of the key parties and assessing the factors which might compel them to negotiate, or prevent them from doing so.

But the idea of negotiation itself needs clarification. The conventional view is that negotiation and conflict are mutually exclusive: antagonists could either fight or talk, and when they talk they no longer seek only to advance their own goals but to look for common solutions with their adversaries. The vast gulf between the goals of the authorities and their opponents suggests that agreement between them to seek solutions is unlikely.

A less demanding view has, however, emerged with the growth of collective bargaining in the country's workplaces. There the partners retain sharply opposing goals even while they negotiate; but they recognise that they cannot eliminate their adversaries and must deal with them if they are to advance towards those goals. Their 'mutual intention of achieving a settlement' and 'willingness to negotiate in spite of the difficulties'[1] stressed by labour relations theory, is based on a strategic assessment of what is required to advance their interests, not on an abstract desire for conciliation.

This may explain why talks between the authorities on the one hand, and community groups and trade unions on the other, have taken place in PWV townships. Despite their hostility to each other, the parties have found that negotiations offered them possibilities for pursuing their interests which would not otherwise have existed. For them, negotiation was not an alternative to wielding power, but the only means of doing so.

The anti-apartheid organisations were too weak to seize power, and so they needed to seek it in other ways; negotiation might also offer them space to re-organise their power base in the face of stringent state security action. For the authorities, negotiation might represent a means

1

of managing conflict without incurring the costs of sustained security action. Both might, therefore, have an interest in negotiation which overrode their hostility to the other. This suggests that negotiation does not require a desire to co-operate with an adversary, but a recognition that it is the only way of pursuing a group's interests; the parties' strategic interests, rather than their view of their adversaries, are thus the motors of negotiation.

But, equally importantly, there are also many examples in which talks have not taken place in spite of an apparent interest in them on both sides; nor did negotiation in the PWV area develop into bargaining in which adversaries backed by organised constituencies forged a permanent relationship in an attempt to wield power through negotiation. This suggests that a latent interest in bargaining makes it more likely, but does not ensure it. This report will, therefore, also examine the factors which impeded negotiation.

Since it is concerned to examine the prospects for negotiation specifically around housing, a brief examination of the housing question and its implications for the adversaries is necessary to place the conflicts examined here in context.

The housing question

An extreme shortage of black residential accommodation, as well as the relatively high price charged for township services, have made housing an issue around which anti-apartheid forces have mobilised. Because most township residents live in houses rented from the authorities, mobilisation has often centred around rent and service charge boycotts; because black local authorities rely on these charges for much of their revenue, these boycotts have, in the 1980s, further undermined their financial stability. Conflict over housing has thus had a directly political flavour, for it has threatened the viability of the official local government system.

The African housing shortage is not a new phenomenon, but it has been growing. The government estimates the present shortage at 500 000 and the national building research institute (NBRI)'s figure is 832 000; the 1980 Venter commission of inquiry estimated the shortage outside 'independent' homelands at about 160 540, noting that the NBRI believed it might be as high as 240 000; it found that some 1,9m new African houses would be needed by the turn of the century[2] — a recent NBRI report estimates that African townships outside the homelands will be short of some 2,7m units by then.[3] Whichever figures are accepted, all the evidence indicates a rapid increase in the backlog.

This shortage obviously places housing at the top of the agenda of township groups seeking to improve their constituents' material conditions: it is also a source of grievance which the authorities have an interest in reducing and this establishes a latent interest in housing negotiation on both sides. This applies not only to formally established townships but to the informal settlements which have mushroomed in many PWV areas in response to the shortage; 'squatter' settlements have been a repeated source of conflict — and negotiation — in many parts of the country and the pressure to find negotiated solutions to their emergence is likely to grow.

But the shortage is only one aspect of the housing question. Equally important is whether township residents are able — and willing — to foot the bill for shelter; rent boycotts are one sign of the meagre financial resources of many residents[4], most of whom are relatively impoverished workers or are unemployed. The provision of shelter is costly and few African residents can afford to cover construction costs or, at least in the view of potential lenders, to afford paying off loans over an extended period.[5] While the government has lifted restrictions on African home ownership it does not propose to build houses itself as it did in the 1950s and 1960s. But few residents can afford the monthly instalments on private homeownership schemes; in 1986 a study of Langa, in the eastern Cape, found that more than 90% of residents could not afford the repayments required for the purchase of a home. [6]

These constraints have prompted conflicts between the authorities and township civic groups, as well as 'squatter' communities, over the cost and provision of shelter; this report will argue that in both cases an impasse has developed between the adversaries. While widespread rent defaulting has continued in several PWV townships, it has prompted neither an end to the state of emergency nor the withdrawal of troops, the major demands of boycott organisers. With some rent defaulters drifting back to the rent offices during 1987, there was growing evidence that the boycott could not be sustained indefinitely.

But the state has been unable to establish the long-term viability or credibility of township local government. Its urbanisation policy, which seeks to limit African settlement in the area, has been contradicted daily as 'squatters' have erected shelter in places of their choice and attempts to remove them have had only limited success. Negotiations around rents and land settlement could offer both sides a way out of the stalemate.

The most immediate evidence of the impasse in formal townships is the rent boycotts; if, of course, they ended, a pressure for negotiation would be removed. But the refusal of township residents to pay rent predates the conflicts of the 1980s; in Soweto, for example, rent increases were resisted twice in the 1970s. The boycotts are thus a symptom of pressures which will recur even if the present actions end. Some official strategists have suggested that African home ownership — in particular selling rented homes to occupants relatively cheaply — could end conflict over rents: but the major component of 'rent' is levies for the provision of infrastructure and services which would still be imposed if this were achieved. Nor is failure to pay rent necessarily a political protest: in townships such as Mamelodi and Atteridgeville, where there were no organised boycotts in 1987, rent defaulting continued spontaneously because a significant number of residents could not afford to pay. These factors suggest that housing costs will remain a source of conflict, and an obstacle to the viability of township local government, regardless of the outcome of present disputes.

Conflicts over the right to settle on land are likely to be even more enduring. The abolition of the pass laws means that the need for land will increasingly be manifested in the cities but there are significant political constraints on the authorities' ability to provide it; although the weakness of 'squatter' organisation is a potential obstacle to bargaining, a deep-rooted deadlock has developed which may only be resolved by negotiation.

These pressures are not uniform throughout the region. Conflict over rents and 'squatting' are spread unevenly through it and in some areas the potential for negotiations is low; in others, it may be the only way in which conflict can be channelled. This report will examine some specific conflicts over housing in an attempt to highlight the practices which have influenced negotiation prospects and to assess their future potential.

The report will discuss five case studies, each of which provides a different insight into the prospects for, and obstacles to, negotiation. The first case study examines a unique negotiated settlement − in Daveyton on the east Rand in 1984. The second discusses conflicts in Tembisa on the east Rand in 1986 and 1987 where a rent boycott met a divided response from the authorities; the opponents of negotiation prevailed. The third study examines Soweto, where negotiations have taken place, only to break down over differing stances on the role of official local authorities in the talks; in this case, constitutional issues intervened to limit negotiation prospects over housing issues despite pressures on both sides to bargain. All three examples provide pointers to the limits and possibilities of housing negotiation.

These examples focus on the costs of shelter as a bargaining issue: but, as already indicated, the lack of it − the most noticeable symptom of which is the growth of informal settlements − may also create pressure for negotiation. While overcrowding in established townships is likely to continue to create potential for instability, the growth of informal settlements has become the most visible constraint to the government's urbanisation policies and has prompted contradictory official responses − attempts to remove settlements have been accompanied by attempts to negotiate with their inhabitants. The report will examine one such settlement, Weiler's Farm, in which talks between the provincial administration and a 'squatter's 'committee', did take place. The example illustrates some of the issues which affect negotiations in informal settlements and the role of political groups in these.

Trade unions have also attempted to resolve housing issues through collective bargaining, a more formal and structured process than the other negotiations discussed. In one case, in the Vaal townships, unions have attempted to settle a rent boycott in this way. Unions and employers have bargained on housing issues in the metal industry; this has been the most advanced form of housing negotiation in the region. These negotiations − and the limitations imposed on them by political factors − will also be discussed.

Finally, the report seeks to use the insights suggested by the case studies to explore strategies to overcome the obstacles to local negotiations over housing issues. It will have achieved its aim if it contributes to a further understanding of — and a negotiated solution to — the shortage of accommodation that haunts the lives of a substantial number of South Africans.

DAVEYTON

September 1984 saw violent conflict — prompted initially by a rent increase — in the townships of the Vaal triangle, initiating 18 months of sometimes violent resistance to black local authorities. But, at the same time, a settlement to a rent conflict in Daveyton, on the east Rand, was being negotiated between community groups, the then department of co-operation and development and the Daveyton council. It showed that, despite growing tensions, the adversaries in the townships could advance their interests through negotiation.

In June, 1984, the Daveyton council announced increases in rents and service charges[7] which were met by a mass protest meeting and demonstrations by supporters of the Sinaba Party, a minority group in the council. In September, Daveyton's mayor, Mr Tom Boya, announced an indefinite suspension of increases, saying that his council would meet community leaders to discuss ways of trimming the budget.[8] Between 1984 and 1987 there was little increase in the rents charged.[9]

The suspension followed talks between the council and a government official on the one hand and two community groups, the Daveyton Action Committee (DAC) and the East Rand People's Organisation (ERAPO), on the other. But accounts of what transpired differ. A member of the DAC, an *ad hoc* group formed to fight the increase, claimed it initially circulated a petition protesting against it which was sent to Dr Piet Koornhof, then minister of co-operation and development. He responded by arranging a meeting between the DAC and the then commissioner for black affairs on the Witwatersrand, a Mr Korff, at which the DAC pointed out irregularities in the council's budgeting and the procedure followed when it promulgated the increases, and demanded that a report to this effect be sent to Pretoria. In September, he added, Mr Boya and the commissioner were called to Pretoria and told not to increase rents.[10]

While DAC members were aware of national political issues, the committee itself did not have an explicitly political profile and this probably made it easier for the authorities to negotiate with it. Most of its members were professional people and their formal education also enabled them to negotiate effectively. But the DAC had little time to organise a significant support base and was therefore too weak to force the authorities to the negotiating table; their decision to talk was prompted, rather, by community pressure.

ERAPO is a United Democratic Front (UDF) affiliate and thus more explicitly committed to political aims, but a spokesman insists that it too was willing to negotiate the abandonment of the increase because this would have helped it boost its organisation in the township. Although it did not take part in the talks with Mr Korff[11], the spokesman says it was jointly responsible for the petition to Dr Koornhof (a DAC member questions this) and to the Benoni city council.[12] Later, he added, the Daveyton council convened a meeting with community leaders, which ERAPO and DAC attended

There were limits to the willingness of both groups to talk. They were weakly organised and feared that they would not be strong enough to exact concessions from the authorities. Their view of the council as a powerless body also made them reluctant to negotiate with it. They thus sought informal talks rather than formal negotiations: at the meeting with councillors, ERAPO said it would not negotiate formally with them and would call for a boycott of rents unless the increases were rescinded.[13]

A council spokesman insists that it pursued a negotiated settlement from the outset. It made several attempts to convene talks with the DAC and ERAPO, but was rebuffed.[14] Later, however, they, together with the Sinaba Party, requested negotiations and this had led to a meeting at which all parties reached an agreement to rescind the increases, which was then made public.[15] These, he said, had been formal negotiations.

A key difference between these accounts concerns the status of talks. But whether they were 'formal' or 'informal' is far less important than the fact that they took place. The factors which prompted the parties to negotiate require examination.

Factors prompting negotiation

The most obvious pressure for negotiation was residents' resistance to the increase. An ERAPO organiser and a council official confirm that thousands attended the protest meeting,[16] and the Sinaba Party's demonstration added to the possibility that the increase could spark conflict. The fact that it was rescinded in September, following the Vaal violence, suggests that the authorities sought to avert similar social conflict in Daveyton.

The DAC's strategy might also have made officials more willing to talk and to withdraw the increase. At its meeting with Mr Korff, it focussed on legal irregularities, arguing that the rentals had been increased without the council consulting residents, as the law required; nor had the minister approved the increases, another legal requirement.[17] The DAC thus relied not on organised power but on holding the council to the law.

It was able to do this firstly because the black local authorities — partly as a result of the unwillingness of people with formal education to serve in them — were often not staffed by people conversant with administrative procedures. Secondly, a DAC member who was an employee of a housing utility company, was familiar with the laws and regulations governing township development.[18] Through the leader of the Sinaba Party, it also obtained minutes of council meetings and other information about its finances. Its members had the skills to analyse the

7

council's budget and legal procedures [19] and to pursue its chosen strategy effectively. [20] At the meeting, the DAC threatened to release evidence of the alleged breach of procedure to the press; this would have embarrassed the authorities and may have prompted them to negotiate the abandonment of the increase.

The DAC's position was also enhanced by its willingness to form an alliance with a group in the council — the Sinaba Party — to gather information it needed to implement its strategy; DAC members attended a ward committee meeting called by Sinaba leader, Mr Shadrack Sinaba,[21] and urged him to provide them with information they needed. It did this despite the presence in its ranks of a member of the black consciousness movement which advocates no 'collaboration' with official local authorities.[22] The DAC thus relied on its strategic expertise rather than grassroots support to achieve a settlement.

According to ERAPO's spokesman, it, too, did not see non-collaboration as a principle: if it could gain from contact with the local authority, it would make contact.[23] But, although he stressed that it was willing to negotiate on rent and housing if this would advance its long-term goals[24], he saw the meeting of short term economic demands as a way of temporary relieving residents' conditions, not as a means to wield power. This may explain why it did not seek more permanent bargaining channels, but was willing to negotiate informally.

The council's policy also helped create a negotiation climate. Unlike many other councillors, Mr Boya has attempted to win support by endorsing some of the demands of his more 'radical' rivals — this may have reduced the community groups' hostility to the council. It also supported negotiation in principle and, according to a spokesman for the mayor, during 1987, the council continued to hold informal discussions with groups such as ERAPO; the mayor had, for example secured the reinstatement of some of its members expelled from school.[25]

This makes Daveyton's council unusual: Mr Boya now leads the United Municipalities of South Africa (UMSA), a breakaway from the more conservative Urban Councils Association of South Africa (UCASA); UMSA believes local authorities should pursue African political demands more vigorously and avoid control by seconded government officials[26] and is thus less hostile to its more militant rivals. But this is still a minority approach among black local councils — most still belong to UCASA — and, in other townships, they have adopted a far more hostile stance toward rival groups: nor might negotiation have resolved the issue had the DAC not shown that the council had ignored correct procedure. And, even in Daveyton, talks fell short of full-scale bargaining.

ERAPO's spokesman insists also that the increase was not thwarted by negotiation but by collective pressure.[27] This assumes, however, that negotiation and pressure are mutually exclusive; but the Daveyton case suggests that negotiation can be — and was — a supplement to pressure. The key question is the circumstances in which negotiation became a means of pursuing ends which could not be achieved by pressure alone.

8

The conflicting parties

The authorities with which community groups negotiated in Daveyton — the council and the department of co-operation and development — were not a monolithic bloc, for the council was not merely an instrument of the government department; it had some autonomy within the confines of the law and used this partially to pursue its own strategy.

The council had been elected in 1983 in a 19,6% poll and only six of the ten wards were contested;[28] it was not representative and this may explain its apparent reluctance at first to meet community demands.[29] But its attempt to win credibility gave it an interest in resolving housing problems and it had the formal power to rescind the increase, thus implementing the outcome of negotiations. (In cases where councils have no formal powers, they could theoretically mediate between community groups and the authorities but this assumes a degree of co-operation between them and their rivals which occurs rarely, if ever.)

The DAC's interest in negotiation has already been discussed; it was increased by the fact that some of its members aspired to local government office, and their participation in a settlement could have helped them achieve that.[30] Nevertheless, its willingness to negotiate was tempered by a perception that the council was relatively powerless to redress the community's grievances and it preferred to negotiate with central government officials who it regarded as the real centre of power.[31]

The officials were reluctant to negotiate — at his meeting with the DAC, Mr Korff was hostile to it[32] — but that they did so is significant. In Daveyton, that decision was probably prompted by a desire to prevent a repetition of the violence which occurred elsewhere — later, other officials were to agree to discussions with eastern Cape UDF officials about township upgrading and administration.

As a minority party in the council, the Sinaba Party appeared to hope that its involvement in the dispute would enhance its electoral support[33]; its chief role was to give the DAC access to information which it needed.

ERAPO's involvement in the dispute is perhaps most significant for it shared the political objectives of other township civic associations. According to its representative, ERAPO clearly had an interest in negotiating a stay of the increases; unemployment was rife amongst its constituency and most residents were unable to afford them.[34] A settlement would enable it to widen its support base by showing that it could win material changes on residents' behalf. But its options were limited by its refusal to give formal recognition to the local authority although this was more a consequence of its belief that the council had no power than a commitment to 'non-collaboration'.[35]

On the other hand, it was willing to talk informally to the council, prompting the latter's spokesman to note that ERAPO and similar groups were opposed in principle to local authorities but were willing, as individuals, to talk to them.[36] This highlights the conflicting pressures to which community groups are subject. Their constituents have a clear interest in housing improvements which could be achieved by

9

negotiation; but they represent a political tradition which has relied on boycotting state structures as a mobilising strategy. The boycott tradition was strengthened during the 1980s as middle class leadership and youth movements, some of whose members have far less interest in resolving housing issues than, say, workers, came to dominate township resistance and to exert significant pressure against 'collaboration' with the authorities. ERAPO was subject to little pressure to avoid negotiation; other civic groups were to face greater pressure.

Although they produced a settlement, the negotiations did not establish a more permanent bargaining relationship between the community groups and the authorities, nor did they build momentum for talks elsewhere on the east Rand. One reason was the weakness of community organisation in the area, despite a strong trade union presence in its factories. Local unionists say that the weakness of community organisation is due to a 'lack of experienced leadership' in community groups. Similarly, the town secretary of Tokoza noted in 1987 that there had been no negotiations because of the lack of support for rent boycotts on the east Rand.[37] A specific cause was security action against community groups; in Daveyton, shortly after the rent issue was resolved, both the DAC's chairman and a unionist who worked for it were detained.[38] Neither ERAPO nor the DAC were strong enough to withstand police action and the DAC ceased to exist after the rent issue was resolved; unionists report that security action similarly 'crushed' community organisation in all townships except Tembisa and Katlehong. Before the police action, ERAPO was preparing to embark on a housing campaign which, it hoped, would end in negotiation with the authorities; it had begun framing housing proposals. But the first state of emergency and the detention of ERAPO leaders halted this initiative.[39]

The negotiations thus represented a short term gain for the community groups which they could not sustain. While ERAPO did hope to negotiate more permanent gains, it seems to have assumed that it could have done so simply by placing a document on officials' desks. But the authorities were likely to negotiate only if they believed they could not impose their own agenda and only strong organisation could have persuaded them of this; although the preconditions for continuing housing negotiation existed in Daveyton, community groups failed to use their breakthrough to win a more permanent say in housing decisions. While residents have benefited from the long period during which no rent increases have been exacted, their control over decisions has grown little. Whether they would be able to resist an increase should the council impose one, is far from clear.

TEMBISA

The DAC used the law to halt a rent increase — similar tactics were later used by other civic groups. Once rent boycotts gathered momentum, several also used the courts to challenge the procedure used to evict boycotters. In at least one township, Tembisa, a community group also tried to use this strategy to bring the local authority to the negotiating table; it hoped to transform discussions between lawyers over legal issues into talks on the issues at stake in the boycott.

The Tembisa rent boycott was called to support a strike in May 1986, by council workers but demands escalated into a call for the removal of troops from the township and the resignation of councillors; the authorities responded by evicting defaulters. The Tembisa civic association (TCA) then threatened to challenge the validity of the evictions in court and this prompted talks between its and the council's lawyers.

The decision to contest the legality of the evictions suggests that some boycott organisers were more pragmatic than those behind calls exhorting residents to 'a life and death decision that we are no longer prepared to finance our own oppression.'[40] Confronted by evictions which threatened their constituents, they opted for legal action to defend them, even though this meant recognising the existence of the council.[41] While rent arrears placed pressure on the council's finances, the evictions confirmed that it retained the power to weaken the boycott and the TCA had to find ways to counter that power.

In July, it twice challenged evictions and in both cases boycotters were reinstated before the matter went to court. But its lawyers knew this strategy could not succeed indefinitely: the council's action could be challenged on procedural grounds only and sooner or later it would follow correct procedure.[42] The legal challenges were designed only to win breathing space for the boycotters and this they did. A similar strategy was used to intervene in another dispute at the same time, prompted by the action of homeless families who moved illegally into empty council houses;[43] shortly after they took occupation some were arrested[44] and the legality of their eviction was again contested by the TCA — again they were not evicted.

But this respite was also a consequence of divisions within the local authority. The resignation of several councillors had prompted the dissolution of the council and its remaining members were appointed administrators of the township. They attempted to defuse conflict by consulting community groups; they also allocated vacant houses to the homeless, shelved plans to evict former hostel dwellers who had occupied houses illegally and announced plans to build more houses. Although this approach was opposed by seconded government officials who later replaced the administrators,[45] the latter's response opened the possibility of a settlement of the dispute while they held office.

The administrators' actions confirmed that black local authorities

11

were not necessarily mere government agents — they did as much to halt evictions as the TCA's legal challenge. During this period, talks did take place between council officials and TCA lawyers — although they soon ended, no evictions occurred until the administrators were replaced.[46] Again the TCA sought to use the law to protect occupants, but again this failed to pressure the council into negotiating an end to the conflict. In 1987, neither legal challenges nor the intervention of white MPs and apparently sympathetic civil servants secured a negotiated settlement; the talks were thwarted by the white officials who were attempting to deal with Tembisa's problems on their own terms.

The administrators and the white officials

The already-mentioned collapse of the council strengthened the TCA's position in theory since, as the council was no longer properly constituted, it could not evict tenants.[47] But evictions continued — white officials took over responsibility for them.

The resigning councillors insisted that they had never been responsible for evictions. The mayor, who resigned in August, cited them as a reason for his decision : the police, he said, over whom the council had no control, were responsible.[48] While this claim is debatable since the Housing Act gave the council the formal power to stop evictions — a power later used by the administrators — it does highlight the ambiguous role of the councillors. They were required to implement government policy by administering the township but, unlike the white officials, they were subject to pressure from residents which made it difficult for them to do this.

The council's collapse seemed to emphasise to the administrators the strength of the opposition they faced. They responded by attempting partly to accommodate the boycotters — they decided that they would not be evicted[49] and, in September, announced that all rents paid from then are to be regarded as instalments on home ownership;[50] according to an administrator, they saw the expansion of the ranks of home owners as a way of depoliticising the housing issue.[51] They also opened talks with the TCA and other township groups in an attempt to resolve the boycott.[52]

They also tried to resolve, through negotiation with community groups, another issue prompted by the housing shortage: demands by the homeless to occupy vacant township land. According to the University of the Witwatersrand based community research group (CRG), 40 000 more people than the township was designed to cater for, lived in Tembisa in 1986[53] — in October a group called the Tembisa working committee (TWC) responded to the housing shortage by arranging for some residents living in overcrowded houses to erect shacks on empty land. It did this after discussions with the chairman of the administrators who allegedly suggested that residents might occupy the land[54] — he confirms that the meetings took place but denies encouraging squatting.[55] Whatever the truth, it is clear from both accounts that the

12

administrators would not have evicted squatters from the land; however, local South African Defence Force (SADF) troops soon evicted them[56] and attempts to negotiate a resolution of this issue suffered the same fate which later befell attempts to settle the boycott.

The administrators' attitude partly reflected the fact that they, unlike the troops — and councillors elsewhere who fled the townships — lived in Tembisa. But their approach to the squatters suggests that they had no plans of their own to house the homeless, despite a stated government willingness to allow controlled self-help housing. [57] Official sanction had been given for more land — in June the minister of constitutional development and planning, Mr Chris Heunis, allocated Tembisa 800ha[58] — but government housing policy prevented the administrators from developing low-cost housing on it.

Government policy now requires households and private developers to play a far greater role in the provision of township housing — the new land was thus owned by two companies, one of which wanted to develop it and then transfer it to the local authority, a step permitted by a recent change to the law.[59] But it was almost impossible for the developers to produce houses which the average resident could afford and the administrators tried to persuade them to sell the land to the government which could then hand it to the local authority; half would be set aside for a self-help scheme which, the chairman of the administrators believed, would be preferable to squatting.[60] This scheme came to nothing, but, even if it had been implemented, the homes would have cost R14 000 to R20 000, beyond the means of most residents. Government policy thus limited the ability of the administrators to resolve the housing problem, despite their sympathy for the homeless.

The administrators were also little more than a supporting cast to the main actors. First, the SADF thwarted a negotiated settlement to the land issue. Then council officials, in alliance with provincial officials, secured the removal of the administrators and began to impose their own solution.

An indication of white officials' attitudes to the administrators is the observation of one that they were influenced by 'political values'[61] — a private developer complains that they were too 'radical.'[62] The officials, led by the town clerk, Mr P Harmse, who was seconded to Tembisa first by the east Rand development board (ERDB) and then by the province, opposed negotiations: he said the council would end the boycott 'even if it means calling the whole SADF to Tembisa'[63] and threatened to counter it by cutting water and electricity supplies.[64]

Unlike the administrators, the seconded white officials, who included police personnel, were a cohesive unit. They had received their grounding in administration boards[65], whose prime task was to implement the pass laws and to control the townships on the government's behalf; they were not used to accommodating residents' demands and saw little need to do so now. They responded to both the land shortage and the boycott with punitive action.

The officials did face pressures: evictions had solved neither the land

13

nor the rents problem and, on the first point, Mr Harmse acknowledged that he was not sure how to regulate the movement of people into Tembisa after the pass laws were repealed. While he would not suggest a return to these laws, he added that 'some sort of control is necessary. The demand is growing and growing. Where will it end?'[66] But they did not believe negotiations could resolve their problem — Mr Harmse said the TCA and similar groups had 'never made constructive recommendations'[67] for the township's problems and could not be a party to their solution.

The armed forces were allies of Mr Harmse and his supporters. The SADF played an active role in evicting boycotters, a strategy which had been first advanced in a document presented to the Lekoa council in 1985 by the joint management centre (JMC) for the Vaal, which advocated selective evictions to end rent boycotts.[68] This was part of a wider approach implemented by the national security management system (NSMS) which aimed also to improve township conditions in a manner calculated to undermine the credibility of 'militant' civic groups. The Vaal document warned against negotiating with 'revolutionary organisations'[69] and this approach was followed in Tembisa too. While factors such as the housing shortage might prevent this strategy from achieving its aims, thereby giving security strategists a potential interest in negotiation, in Tembisa these constraints were not yet strong enough to prompt a willingness to deal with civic groups.

This approach was the key obstacle to negotiation after the council's collapse in August. The TCA had then instructed its lawyers to initiate talks with the council's lawyers on the issues which prompted the boycott. On 1 September, they proposed that the boycott be ended if rent were reduced to 'affordable levels', pensioners were exempted, the quality of houses and services were improved and the council opened its financial statements to inspection[70]; the council's lawyers rejected the proposals.[71] The administrators had been in office for only two weeks and had little time to consolidate their formal powers. It seems likely, then, that this outright rejection was prompted by the officials, a view supported by Mr Harmse's warning at the time that families who had regained occupation of their houses would be evicted again if they did not pay rent[72]; some weeks later it was reported that he again urged evictions but was opposed by the administrators.[73] In a later interview he stressed that negotiation could not end the boycott: 'Ninety per cent of it is because of intimidation, not because people have grudges against the council or the government.'[74] Neither did the local JMC consider negotiation with the TCA.[75]

Indeed, while the administrators were assuring squatters that they could continue occupying vacant houses, JMC meetings — which were reportedly attended by local headmasters as well as police and officials — were taking place daily to discuss a counter — strategy which included evictions.[76] It was only a matter of time before the administrators, who lacked a support base in the township, would be eclipsed by this counter force.

The ostensible reason for the administrators' removal was that it was demanded by dissatisfied council workers. But the chairman of the administrators insists that it followed tensions between them and the officials, partly prompted by his demand that the latter be replaced by Africans.[77] He alleges that the officials worked actively to remove the administrators and that matters came to a head when he and Mr Harmse were called to provincial headquarters in an apparent attempt to resolve the dispute: some weeks later the administrators were suspended. Whatever the immediate reason for this decision, it is clear that the approach of the officials and the administrators conflicted and that the former's triumphed.

Tensions between white officials and African councillors were not restricted to Tembisa: a recent study[78] reveals that white development board officials felt threatened by the transfer of their formal powers to African councillors in 1983 and a second study[79] reports repeated conflicts between the boards and African local authorities once these were established because board officials were seen by the African councillors to be effectively controlling the councils. This makes it even more likely that officials would seek to remove administrators who acted independently.

Once the officials took over, eviction orders were served on squatters occupying vacant houses. TCA lawyers held talks with the local SADF and police, as well as the minister of police, all of whom denied issuing the notices. The lawyers than asked two opposition MPs, Mrs Helen Suzman and Mr Peter Soal, to negotiate a reprieve with Mr Heunis. The minister, apparently convinced of the need to negotiate a solution, sent a message through the director of local government, Mr L Koch, asking the Tembisa authorities not to proceed[80] — he also apparently asked them to meet TCA lawyers once the white administrator was appointed. In June, the lawyers met this official, who indicated that squatters would be evicted — the lawyers protested that this contradicted Mr Koch's message and demanded a meeting at which he would be present. Mr Koch claimed he had received no report from the Tembisa authorities on the progress of talks.[81] From June 23, the squatters were arrested and fined.[82]

These incidents suggest division between the department of constitutional development and the officials and security forces — similar differences appeared in other townships at the time. Events in Tembisa suggest that there are indeed sections of officialdom and black local authorities who accept the need to negotiate a solution to housing conflicts, but that they face significant opposition from security strategists whose view continues to dominate. Future negotiating possibilities will depend partly on whether the former view is strengthened.

Since the officials took over, sporadic evictions have continued. But so too have the boycott and illegal occupations; thus, while the anti-negotiation faction within officialdom remains dominant in Tembisa, potential pressure for negotiation continues.

15

SOWETO

In Tembisa, officials did not acknowledge that a deadlock between them and community groups gave them an interest in negotiation. In Soweto, a similar deadlock in 1986 and 1987 did prompt negotiation: while it has not produced a settlement, the pressures which impelled repeated talks between the Soweto council and its adversaries require discussion.

Like the TCA, the Soweto civic association (SCA) used the law to challenge the eviction of rent defaulters — at least five legal actions were launched in 1986 and 1987.[83] But they were also accompanied by negotiations: there were 17 reported cases of talks between the Soweto council and community groups. Another contrast with Tembisa was that the official willingness to talk was prompted by the white town clerk, not councillors.

Perceptions of the parties

The approach of the town clerk, Mr Nico Malan, differed markedly from that of his counterpart in Tembisa. He stressed that black local authorities are forced to deal with political issues as they are the only official political platform for urban Africans.[84] Their first task was to negotiate with community groups to 'determine the needs of the people'[85] and to present proposals raised at these talks to the government. As an example, he said, the Soweto council had successfully urged the authorities to reduce the price of rented houses sold to tenants because it believed that complaints that houses had not been properly maintained over the years were justified.[86] It had also urged consultants re-examining the guide plan for the central Witwatersrand to set aside land for two more cities, each the size of Soweto[87] because, by the end of 1988, the last available residential stands in Soweto would be developed and, due to physical limitations, the township could not expand sideways. Towards the end of the century 50 000 more stands would be needed to cope with the existing backlog as well as the needs of shack-dwellers[88] — and the only solution was to develop new townships.

This concern for upgrading is consistent with the security strategy outlined earlier: the Soweto local authority is assisted by a JMC which had, according to Mr Malan, helped it to improve services such as refuse removal.[89] But this JMC did not oppose negotiations with civic groups[90] as long as these addressed civic issues and aimed at meeting the material needs of residents.[91] Unlike some other JMCs, it also did not attempt to bypass the local council, which continued to make policy.

Mr Malan's position on negotiation was not simply rhetorical: in May, there were negotiations between the council and SCA lawyers who challenged the confiscation of the possessions of tenants who had been evicted from council houses[92]; later there were talks with street committee leaders in White City who wanted the eviction of rent defaulters halted.[93] According to Mr Malan, the council recognised that civic groups could contribute to solving housing problems — he had contacted the SCA because it could play an important role in resolving housing issues.[94]

The SCA was not the only civic group with which the council held talks: in 1986 and 1987, it met the Soweto electricity advice centre (SEAC) seven times. The SEAC was formed in 1983 to oppose a rise in electricity tariffs and what it saw as excessive electricity charges. It monitors these charges as well as other housing-related issues and enjoys support from prominent community figures, such as Mrs Sally Motlana[95] — Azanian Peoples' Organisation (AZAPO) officials also claim close contact with it[96], noting that it provided important potential for linking short term civic campaigns with long term political objectives. This stance is significant as AZAPO has generally opposed negotiation with the authorities on civic issues.

Discussions between the SEAC and the council centred not only around electricity but rents, service charges, home ownership, housing subsidies, land availability, the legitimacy of the Black Local Authorities Act and the eviction of rent boycotters.[97] That these talks developed into substantive negotiations is illustrated by a meeting at which the council proposed that sites in Soweto be sold for R670, that rent be reduced by R15 and that upgrading charges be abolished. The SEAC proposed that sites be sold for at most R50-R100; that the functions of the council's electricity department be centralised; and that service charges be determined jointly by it (i.e the SEAC), the council, the Rand Water Board, the Electricity Supply Commission and the Johannesburg city council.[98] One meeting — in April 1987 — was attended by Mr Willem Cruywagen, administrator of the Transvaal.[99] The final meeting between the council and the SEAC took place on 3 August 1987 to discuss electricity charges;[100] councillors attended this meeting (only officials had attended earlier ones) which indicated that the SEAC, unlike many other civic groups, was prepared to deal with them.

The SEAC, like the DAC, had the technical knowledge to negotiate effectively — a second similarity was that it has no political affiliations. Again, both factors may have aided negotiation. But, unlike the DAC, the SEAC had no mandate to negotiate on residents' behalf and it also had no organised support base. This limited the negotiations and may have helped ensure that they failed to resolve the issues discussed. Their significance, rather, was that they showed the way forward to the SCA.

Besides these meetings, there was also contact between lower echelon council employees and advice workers affiliated to the Advice Centres Association (ACA). Like the SEAC, the ACA had no organised constituency: its affiliates provided free para-legal services and advice on community issues to township residents.[101] This limited the importance of the talks — they would have become significant only had it developed a constituency. But both it and the SEAC were raising issues of concern to groups who did have a following and supporters of both the UDF and AZAPO, including three AZAPO executive members, worked for ACA advice centres.[102] Their talks with the council could, therefore, have been catalysts to negotiations between it and these groups.

While the SEAC raised demands shared by the civic groups, the ACA raised individual grievances only.[103] They included charges of corruption against council officials, conflicting claims between residents over the right to occupy a house and the right of an evicted tenant to re-occupy a house and to have goods confiscated by the authorities returned.[104] Despite their limited scope, these contacts with the council might have allowed the advice centres to win residents' confidence and build an organised base which could have won more substantial concessions in further negotiations: in the deadlock which existed in Soweto, they might have had a scope for organisation which civic groups, constrained by security action, did not have.

Another group of organisations which dealt with the council and could have provided a catalyst for negotiation were the Agency for Industrial Mission (AIM) and the Witwatersrand Network for the Homeless (WNH), both based at the church-sponsored Wilgespruit fellowship centre: employees of the centre helped residents of flats in Jabulani, who negotiated with the council in March 1987 over the rent boycott, to prepare their demands. These negotiations differed from those in which the ACA and SEAC took part in two important ways. Firstly, it was the residents themselves who negotiated. Secondly, the Wilgespruit employees were associated with the Black Consciousness (BC) movement. The talks were therefore, albeit indirectly, an example of negotiation between the authorities and their political adversaries over material issues.

The deadlock between the authorities and United Democratic Front (UDF) affiliates gave BC groups — whose popular appeal had waned since the early 1980s — an opportunity to intervene to break the logjam; the only way they could do this was by facilitating negotiations, a role which conflicted with BC's insistence that the authorities be boycotted on principle. They were thus forced by events to rethink the relationship between short- and long-term goals. This willingness to advance tactical goals through negotiation was also developing, albeit in a different context, within the SCA.

The BC activists justified their stance by distinguishing between political and civic groups; for the former, negotiations with state officials were not an option, but for the latter they were. They recognised that civic groups would find it difficult to operate effectively if they emphasised a particular political approach; a WNH representative said that civic organisations tended to be local, mass-based, movements whose members could support different political groups: like trade unions, they had to be issue-orientated[105] and this might imply negotiations with the authorities. By aiding Jabulani residents, the activists hoped to persuade them to see their rent fight as a part of a broader political battle and build a base for organisation which would look beyond negotiations over rents to wider issues.[106] This approach had

18

been adopted at AZAPO's 1984 conference, which decided to contribute to building township organisations around material issues: the community organisations would remain non- aligned towards the major political groups and would also use negotiation to pursue short-term goals.[107] Despite their opposition to 'collaboration', the BC activists acknowledged, therefore, that negotiations over urban issues could advance their political goals — according to a WNH activist, it was they who urged Jabulani residents to negotiate with the council.

Negotiations did take place between the council and Jabulani representatives[108] and an immediate outcome was an undertaking from the council that evicted flat dwellers could return pending a final settlement. But residents also raised longer-term issues, such as alternative housing. Had they been able to negotiate these with the council, they would have gained an important source of organised power over local development decisions — this prospect was consistent with the activists' aim of building organisation and gave them an interest in encouraging the talks. The negotiations obviously implied some form of recognition of the council by the negotiators but the Wilgespruit group, like other political groups in Soweto, was beginning to argue that civic associations had a distinct role which could be hampered by the non-collaborationism stressed at the national level: it was this awareness, together with the reformist stance of the Soweto authorities, which made negotiation possible.

This new stance was also reflected in the involvement of the Wilgespruit groups in a dispute between African and white residents of Crown Mines, on Johannesburg's fringes, and Rand Mines Properties (RMP), which owned the suburb and wished to demolish it. After negotiations with RMP, it agreed to demolish only half the area, to upgrade reprieved houses and to set some aside for African residents. While some residents did lose their homes, the agreement represented an advance. Initially, resistance to the demolition had been hampered by residents' belief that they were powerless to challenge the company but a residents' committee was organised and they gained a growing sense of their own power to achieve a settlement which at least partly met their needs.[109]

This willingness to attempt to build power by pursuing negotiable short-term demands had also grown in groups such as the SCA. Unlike the east Rand groups, it had retained a presence in the township despite the detention of several leaders. It had also developed grassroots structures which, in theory, gave it an organisational base which they lacked. According to an SCA representative, by 1987 it had organised most of its members into street committees, which comprised representatives of houses in a street. They elected two members to serve on a 'block committee' which met weekly and also sent delegates to a branch committee (the SCA's White City branch committee was to hold talks with the Soweto town clerk) which in turn sent members to a zone committee.[110] It is unclear how many residents were active in these structures or whether they were fully accountable to their constituents.

19

But they did offer the SCA a far greater prospect than the other civic groups of both surviving and wielding power under hostile conditions.

But the SCA had failed to prompt the collapse of the council and was forced, if it wanted to make short-term gains, to interact with it. It also faced pressure from its constituents to defend them against eviction and thus to resolve the boycott — this inevitably implied talks with the council. This was not lost on SCA leaders. They had held preliminary talks with Mr Malan; although these had not resolved the impasse, they believed they had been useful and there was a growing feeling that 'perhaps we need to seriously take that option (negotiation)'.[111]

The SCA's growing commitment to negotiation was also prompted by a belief that the authorities would retain an interest in negotiating with it. While it believed the state might respond to the boycott by giving rented houses away, this would not end the dispute as the council would still have to collect service charges and would remain a potential target for boycotters. If this did happen, an SCA representative said, it could negotiate over the level of these charges.[112] SCA officials accepted Mr Malan's commitment to negotiation — prompted in their view by the failure of security action to end the boycott — and believed it was shared by some other state officials.[113] While the SCA had not yet decided whether it wanted to restrict talks to the boycott or to raise the future upgrading of Soweto as well[114] it had accepted the need for negotiations on the former.

The SCA's stance on negotiation did not depend only on its officials' views. Militant youth groups had played the major role in enforcing the boycott and they remained opposed to negotiation. But SCA officials believed that the emergence of grassroots SCA structures was making it a more powerful force than the youth groups,[115] a view partly vindicated in April 1987, when the UDF, to which the SCA was affiliated, advocated talks between the authorities and civic associations to resolve the rent issue.[116] It did not urge negotiations with the black local authorities, but its statement indicated that it too now recognised that negotiation over material demands did not weaken its political goals. In 1987, then, both local state officials and their adversaries in Soweto had accepted that the provision of affordable housing was a priority and that it should be negotiated. But negotiation still faced an important stumbling block - the status of the Soweto councillors.

Despite their willingness to negotiate, both the BC activists and the SCA retained their opposition to talks with councillors - both on principle and because they were seen to be powerless: the UDF had made it clear that it was advocating talks with Mr Malan, who was seen to represent the government. But Mr Malan insisted that, as a council employee, he could not bypass the councillors who formally employed him. This difference was ultimately to become the chief block to negotiation in Soweto.

In the short term new ideas for breaking the logjam were emerging. In December 1986, the SEAC called for a halt to 'all threats and eviction orders' until a solution to the boycott was negotiated.[117] AZAPO suggested that the boycott could be ended if the state gave away houses to people who had been living in them for 30 or more years and that service charges be subsidised 'on the same basis as in the white suburbs'; it said it would encourage a residents committee (or similar body) to negotiate these demands with the authorities.[118] This demand suggested a lack of expert knowledge of the workings of local government but also indicated a strategic rethink which was vital to the creation of a negotiating climate.

But the new commitment to negotiation remained limited. Besides opposition to talking to councillors, AZAPO activists still believed that the successful settlement of civic conflicts could result in residents losing sight of political goals. AZAPO had thus decided to encourage civic groups to escalate their demands rather than to present only those which the authorities might concede - while it recommended that they raise demands which could be met it urged them also to add some which could not. The meeting of some demands, it believed, would relieve residents' material situation − but if all were met political militancy would be defused. And, if some were not met, this would reveal the 'undemocratic nature of the apartheid state' to residents.[119] They were therefore as concerned to limit the success of talks as to encourage them.

In practice, these reservations came to centre on one issue: the status of the councillors. And their effect was that all the civic groups who now supported negotiation in principle, continued to baulk at talking to councillors. It was this view, together with Mr Malan's insistence that councillors should take part in talks, which became the decisive obstacle to negotiation.

Limitations on the negotiations

The talks in Soweto in 1986 and 1987 did not resolve the major points of dispute and, in only 7 of the 17 reported contacts between the council and community groups, were issues of importance to the rent conflict settled. The reinstatement of evicted residents was negotiated four times, and SCA lawyers, backed by the threat of court action, negotiated an end to confiscation of evictees' possessions (in most cases, however, legal action led to court rulings rather than negotiations). A community group also negotiated a reprieve for and the upgrading of an area threatened with demolition and an advice centre negotiated the settlement of a family dispute with the council. Six of the seven talks between the council and the SEAC failed to reach agreement and the seventh merely produced a council acknowledgement that residents' complaints about high electricity charges were valid. In general, the talks seldom advanced beyond a presentation of opposing views.[120]

A key obstacle to the SEAC talks was a sharp difference in views on who should foot the bill for land, housing and services; the SEAC's ombudsman, Mr Bernard Moleke, stressed residents' limited ability to afford these while Mr Malan emphasised the council's need to recover costs from them.[121] And, while Mr Malan suggested that the government and the Johannesburg city council be asked to finance Soweto's upgrading only, the SEAC demanded that they subsidise existing charges as well.[122] These differences were illustrated at their fourth meeting, when Mr Malan proposed that the council sell land at R670 per site. Mr Moleke replied that residents could not afford this: 'One of the main reasons why rent is being boycotted, I said, is that people say they cannot buy the land they claim is theirs. He said: "This is the language of the radicals." I said I stay in Soweto and everybody is saying it.'[123]

The SEAC believed that the state should meet the costs of housing land, Mr Malan insisted that land and services had an economic cost which residents should meet. So deep was this difference that it almost caused the collapse of the talks. At a meeting in February, 1987, Mr Moleke reiterated the demand that sites and houses should be given to occupants because they had been paying rent for 30 to 40 years. Mr Malan replied by 'telling me that I should leave his office and that we must never talk again until we have seen the respective ministers, because whenever I come to his office I only "demand, demand, demand." He said I did not believe in give and take.'[124] Although they did talk again — confirming the pressures on both sides to negotiate — this difference also proved an obstacle to negotiations between local authorities and other civic groups.

Community groups believe the council was forced to insist that residents foot the bill because it did not have the resources to do so itself. Mr Malan replied that the council was able to buy land, install services and erect houses by borrowing money from the national housing commission.[125] But he did concede that it did not have the money to implement housing projects.[126] This is illustrated by the fact that participants in its site-and- service schemes had to pay R6 000 in cash to meet the cost of land and services.[127] The insistence that residents pay as much of the cost of services as possible is also a key element of government policy. It first insisted that African local authorities raise revenue from residents: the introduction of regional services councils (RSCs) marked a change in this policy because RSCs are to raise revenue by taxing business and use this to provide township infrastructure. But local authorities still lack the financial resources to redress popular grievances.

These constraints not only limited the ability of the Soweto talks to produce a solution; community groups also insist that they are a key reason for their reluctance to negotiate with councils. The SCA thus argued that it could not negotiate a solution to Soweto's housing problems with the council because it simply did not have the means to solve them.[128] Similarly, the ACA argued that black local authorities did not have the power to meet housing demands.[129] It is, of course, precisely the council's inability to resolve the housing issue which has prompted its willingness to negotiate it — but, in the view of community groups, this willingness is of limited value as long as councils do not have the resources to implement a settlement.

This perception did not prevent the community groups from

negotiating with Mr Malan. When, however, he insisted that councillors take part in the talks, this proved an insurmountable stumbling block. In August, talks between the council and Pimville residents broke down when the latter objected to the presence of four councillors[130] and, increasingly, the local authority's insistence that councillors be present at talks and community groups' refusal to accept this, became an obstacle to further contact. But neither Mr Malan nor other officials could agree to bypass the councillors because to do so would have been to deny the legitimacy of black local authorities which the government had created. Evidence of this gulf was provided when the SEAC's Mr Moleke demanded the abolition of the Black Local Authorities Act. This, he said, 'shocked' Mr Malan. 'He was plainly riled... He said this meant that he should cut the throat of his employer. I insisted that it was still the best solution. Anger was written all over his face with this suggestion.'[131]

Had the community groups commanded enough organised power to force the authorities to abandon the councils, this difference may not have obstructed negotiations. But they did not and the status of councillors became the issue on which talks foundered. This difference may remain a constraint on housing negotiation until either the community groups decide that their limited power forces them to reach a temporary accomodation with the local authorities or events prompt the government to retreat significantly from its commitment to them. But this constraint applies only in areas where local authorities already exist; in informal settlements, where they do not, differences over the local government system need not obstruct negotiation.

INFORMAL SETTLEMENTS

Rent boycotts may prove to be only temporary phenomena; but another pressure on government housing policy, the growth of informal settlements around the major cities, will almost certainly persist, undermining official urbanisation policy and creating negotiation possibilities.

Before July 1986, the pass laws were the authorities' chief instrument for preventing 'squatting'. While their success was limited, in the post-pass law era, the instruments of control have become even less effective and many African people have been able to implement their own solutions to overcrowded and costly shelter. But conflicts have emerged as the authorities challenge their right to remain on land where they have settled.

In the PWV as in other areas, the state, as it did in the 1950s and 1960s,[132] has sought to prevent the homeless erecting shelter outside its control. In the earlier period, it sought to do this by erecting segregated mass housing estates and forcibly moving 'squatters' who qualified in terms of the pass laws to them. But, in the 1980s, it has become increasingly impractical to shift informal settlements and the repeal of the pass laws has removed many of the weapons the government used to do this. Negotiations with squatter leaders to determine the conditions under which they might remain on the land may therefore be the only means by which the authorities can ensure that urbanisation in the post-pass law era remains orderly.[133]

The government's post-1986 urbanisation policy included plans to prevent the concentration of people in the major cities by encouraging industrial decentralisation: in 1986, the state president, Mr PW Botha, said this required the creation of conditions in which the 'quality of life' and 'stability' in the cities could be maintained and that urbanisation itself should be decentralised.[134] The supply of residential land in the cities would thus be limited[135] to promote 'balanced' development between urban and rural areas[136] thus frustrating the land needs of thousands of Africans in the PWV area, whose numbers continued to grow after the pass laws were repealed.

There is thus a contradiction between the stated aims of the new urbanisation policy and the means chosen to implement it. The goal is orderly African settlement — yet the means deny them land where it is most needed to achieve this. The continued stress on limiting city land, together with the racial land zoning imposed by the Group Areas Act, have ensured that the abolition of the pass laws has not been accompanied by a willingness to open sufficient land in the metropolitan areas to Africans. In the absence of the old controls, many homeless people simply occupied land, and the authorities frequently sought to remove them.

According to the new policy, local authorities would be instructed to establish serviced sites for new arrivals to the cities. Yet black local authorities generally lacked the expertise to administer self-help schemes and feared that unconventional housing would encourage squatting. Armed with greater powers under the Slums Act and the Prevention of Illegal Squatting Act, they often sought to curb or remove informal settlements, but rarely have they provided an alternative to them. The result has not been 'orderly urbanisation' but clashes between squatters and municipal police.

But not all official responses inhibit orderly urbanisation. The squatting law also now allows the authorities to allocate land for 'controlled squatting'[137] and attempts to remove informal settlements have been accompanied by several 'reprieves' for squatter communities. In the PWV, controlled squatting has been permitted in Soweto.[138] This implies a limited acknowledgment that informal settlements must be countenanced which has prompted negotiations between squatters and the provincial administration.

Official acceptance of 'controlled squatting' need not imply a willingness to negotiate the terms of land occupation with squatter communities. In the western Cape, the growth of areas set aside for 'controlled squatting' in Khayelitsha has been achieved largely by violence in the Crossroads squatter camp, prompted by divisions in the community, which drove many former residents to the new area.[139] In the eastern Cape, a forced removal from the township of Langa preceded the setting up of a controlled squatting settlement at KwaNobuhle.[140] But acceptance of the principle does, at least, open the possibility of negotiation which might recognise the permanence of informal settlements. More importantly, the pressures which face official policy towards informal settlements have forced the authorities to mix attempts to remove 'squatters' with efforts to accommodate them. These pressures may increasingly prompt officials to negotiate with squatter communities.

Squatting and land use in the PWV

The rise of informal settlements in the PWV area has taken two forms. In the established townships, tens of thousands of backyard shacks have become a permanent feature and their emergence has prompted tensions between occupants and local authorities. But it has been primarily the growth of informal dwellings on vacant land, often outside a local authority area, which has posed the most immediate challenge to government urbanisation policy: in 1987, government sources estimated that there were 850 000 squatters in the Transvaal.[141] The majority of these were living in settlements in the PWV, if one excluded Winterveld, the sprawling settlement to the north east of Pretoria.

The growth of these settlements first became evident in the mid-1970s and is the consequence of policies adopted over several decades. Squatters included people entitled to live in the cities by the pass laws but who could not find approved housing, farm workers forced to leave the land when farmers reduced their workforce and, latterly, newcomers from the homelands. According to a representative of what was the largest shack-dweller community in the region (it comprised about 1 200 shacks in 1987[142]), Weiler's farm, near Walkerville, south of Johannesburg, it has existed since the 1930s. But numbers grew sharply from the late 1970s when farms in the area were expropriated to make way for Indian townships around Lenasia: former farm workers moved to the 'squatter' areas as did pensioners from the Vaal and Soweto, who could not afford rent.[143]

Informal settlements have also emerged elsewhere in the PWV. By 1983, there were about 35 000 shacks in the vicinity of Katlehong on the east Rand;[144] many were demolished, but, by March 1987, 500 families were reported to be squatting in the township[145] and by August the number was said to have grown to 1 300.[146] Other east Rand areas where squatting was reported in 1987 were Tokoza, Varkfontein (near Benoni) and KwaThema[147] and west Rand areas included Bekkersdal, Dobsonville, Big Farm, near Roodepoort, Wilgespruit, and Westonaria.[148] In Soweto, the main squatter settlements were at Mshenguville and Protea South, while 60 squatters were reported to be living in Nancefield. A squatter settlement also arose on Johannesburg's northern perimeter near Honeydew.[149] The Weiler's farm representative also reported settlements in at least ten Vaal areas.[150] None of these areas has been set aside by the government for residential use. While it has allocated land in the PWV for African housing, this is not sited where it is most needed. Settlements thus arose in places chosen by squatters themselves.

Because the government can no longer remove 'squatters' from the cities, it has sought to curb informal settlements by finding approved land for their inhabitants. But official land use policies, enshrined in binding guide plans which demarcate areas for settlement, have made little provision for new land and, in some areas, it has been forced to alter these significantly. In the townships around Pretoria, for example, 1984 directives which sharply limited land availability[151] were contradicted by the setting aside of some 3 000ha in or around the townships. The 1984 east Rand guide plan emphasised the 'infilling' of existing townships rather than the creation of new ones.[152] Since its publication, 30 000 new sites have been set aside for residential purposes but have been earmarked mainly for conventional private market housing. The central Witwatersrand draft guide plan recommended in 1986 that portions of the farm Diepsloot (near Midrand) be set aside for a new township[153] but, in the face of opposition, the government has not implemented the plan and has commissioned a study to identify housing land in the area.

The authorities have thus been forced to retreat from earlier land use policies. But a variety of pressures, chief among them white opposition to new African settlements, have prevented them setting aside the land they need if they are to control the growth of informal settlements. Nowhere was this more evident than in the Vaal triangle. In 1982, the

Vaal river complex guide plan set aside the farm Wildebeesfontein to the north of Sebokeng for a new African township.[154] But all the west Rand and Vaal squatter settlements fell outside this area and the policy could be implemented only by moving them, a process which, if imposed by force, might be anything but orderly.

Where they have attempted to force the inhabitants of some settlements to move, they have had limited success. In 1983, about 65 000 squatters were evicted by development board police[155] but the re-emergence of squatting around Katlehong and Tokoza showed that as long as houses were scarce, informal settlements would reappear. Action against squatters continued in 1987 in Tokoza, Bekkersdal, Kagiso and Roodepoort[156] where the city council repeatedly demolished shacks[157] but failed to remove 'squatters' who simply rebuilt their shacks: in late 1987, the provincial administration acknowledged the need to accommodate them by allocating them nearby land.

Squatters were compelled to resist eviction by the shortage of land and relatively high cost of formal housing near their place of work; the alternative to resistance is often homelessness. Some, in areas such as Westonaria and old Lenasia, had thus devised novel ways to avoid detection: they dismantled their shelters during the day and rebuilt them at night. 'Some keep blankets in the dustbins. You just see dustbins turned over like that, and underneath is the blankets, clothing, and things like that.'[158] This resistance made it increasingly difficult for the authorities to impose control.

The response of local authorities to the impasse has often differed from that of provincial officials. While the province, responsible for urbanisation policy in the whole region, has an interest in accommodating some informal settlements, some (but not all) local authorities have sought to limit squatting within their boundaries. In 1986/87, the Soweto council demolished shacks in several areas, assisted at times by security forces — in July, its plans to destroy 1 000 shacks on Macdonald's farm were not implemented after the provincial and central authorities and an opposition MP, Mr Rupert Lorimer, intervened.[159] Conversely, it was usually Transvaal provincial administration (TPA) officials who approached squatters as negotiators.

In some areas, attempts by the TPA to negotiate have been accompanied by attempts by the security forces to harrass informal settlements. Thus Weiler's Farm residents negotiated a stay of eviction with provincial officials in 1987 — but had earlier been raided by police and SADF troops who demolished several half completed structures.[160] In April, after a 'reprieve' was granted by the province, troops set up a roadblock at the entrance to the camp, confiscated residents' goods and allegedly beat some of them.[161] The TPA's attitude to these actions is unclear, since they did strengthen its bargaining position. But its actions did imply that security action alone could not control informal settlements and that negotiation might be a means to this; limited negotiations did take place between squatters and the authorities at Weiler's Farm and in Soweto.

Limited negotiations

While local authorities had a greater incentive than the province to move squatter camps, they also had an interest in reaching a *modus vivendi* with their inhabitants. Doing so might increase their credibility among residents and the erection of informal dwellings relieved congestion in existing houses. Thus, in 1986 and 1987, the Soweto council also negotiated with inhabitants of informal settlements under its jurisdiction. In August 1986 it met the Fred Clarke squatters residents committee to discuss the provision of houses and sites and in January 1987 it met 50 Mshenguville squatters to negotiate their right to occupy the land on which they had settled[162] — in November, the shack dwellers committee reportedly met the state president to negotiate the provision of serviced sites.[163] In April, it again met Mshenguville squatters to negotiate their relocation to a council-controlled site-and-service camp.[164]

It was not clear who negotiated on behalf of the squatters or whether the negotiators had a firm mandate from residents. But attempts to organise and unite squatters have often failed; although they are united in their need for shelter, they are competing for the right to occupy limited land and communities have often split into opposing groups. At times the authorities have been able to split informal settlements by making agreements with some residents at the expense of others.

The negotiations yielded limited gains for the two settlements. The Fred Clarke group and the council agreed that it would allow them to buy serviced sites or core houses elsewhere in the township, but it later transpired that more than half the sites offered were sold to other parties.[165] The Mshenguville talks were followed three days later by further evictions but, in January 1987, the council agreed to allow squatters to stay until other housing was provided — in return the squatter delegation agreed that no new shacks would be erected.[166] In April the parties agreed that squatters would move to a site-and-service scheme elsewhere in Soweto.[167] These agreements were a limited advance for the squatters, but a significant one for the council which was able to bring the settlements under control by relocating residents to site-and-service schemes;[168] the terms of the agreement appear to have reflected weak organisation within the two settlements.

At Weiler's Farm, the first meeting between the TPA and the squatter committee took place in February 1987, after the TPA expropriated the land on which the settlement stood prior to declaring it an emergency camp in terms of new squatting regulations, a step which was at least a partial recognition of squatters' right to stay. Other meetings were held later.

Their primary aim was to discuss the exercise of TPA control over the area — which it assumed after it was declared an emergency camp — and in particular its desire that a local authority be constituted.[169] Although residents were granted only a 'temporary' reprieve pending their removal to an area allocated for housing by the guide plan, the local authority plan implied that at least some would remain on the farm. But it also created potential for division within the community between supporters and opponents of the local authority system: similar plans had that effect in other informal settlements. The TPA also said it wanted to prevent 'uncontrolled' trading in the camp by issuing trading licenses[170] this indicated an official desire to bring the area under TPA, rather than residents', control. The squatter committee responded by raising the role of troops in the area, the provision of water and other grievances. A meeting in September discussed the level of site-and-service charges and a suggestion by some committee members that the TPA's plans to upgrade the camp be negotiated.171

These talks did not result in greater formal squatter control over decisions, nor did they address the central issue, their right to live permanently on the farm. On the first score, the TPA insisted it would be responsible for 'solving' squatter's problems and that regulations would be published setting site- and-service charges, introducing traders' licenses and providing for schooling.[172] On the second it implied that residents would be allowed to stay only until funds were found to install infrastructure on the land to which they were to be moved.[173] But the authorities appeared to have conceded the right of some residents to stay; if they do attempt to move others, this may provide scope for more substantive negotiation — but could also prompt similar divisions to those which beset other informal settlements.

This highlights the tensions implict in negotiation between the authorities and squatters. The potential for division within informal settlements gives the authorities an incentive to negotiate the terms of settlement with some residents groups only, thus excluding others and limiting settlement. But they can do so only by conceding to some the right to remain where they are, thus partly weakening their control over land allocation. Weiler's Farm was the only informal settlement in the region which had been recognised — albeit temporarily — by the TPA, and the pressures on official urbanisation policy suggest that a settlement of the key issue, the right to remain, will be reached. But experience in other areas suggests that this might be extended only to those residents willing to co-operate with the authorities. This would be prevented only if the settlement's leaders are able to build organisation strong enough to overcome not only the potential threat of security action but also that of divisions among residents, which had already begun to emerge in response to the TPA's local authority and upgrading plans.

For Weiler's Farm residents, organisation was a relatively new phenomenon and it appears to have taken root only to a limited extent. The committee was formed in 1983, after squatters began settling en masse. It was said to have represented all the squatters but the extent of community participation in and control of it is unclear. According to a committee member, its first act had been to find, with the help of the Black Sash, a lawyer who, in an attempt to halt action against residents by the police, wrote to the authorities arguing that they might not have the right to evict squatters until other housing was provided. These were met only by assurances that 'the matter was receiving attention' until February 1987 when the issue was referred to the TPA.[174] From 1984, the committee also demanded that the authorities recognise the settlement's permanence and negotiate the terms of its upgrading[175] but received no response. It is not clear whether the committee saw legal intervention as a substitute for organisation, but it does not seem to have complemented it with attempts to build organisation.

The need for organisation was highlighted by a further factor influencing the authorities — pressure from white residents in Walkerville for the removal of Weiler's Farm. This had been building for some time before it became an emergency camp and the TPA's decision may have been designed to reassure white voters of its willingness to control the area. This pressure persists, giving the authorities an added incentive to impose control by moving some residents elsewhere: since the expropriation, white residents have been holding protest meetings and circulating a petition which was to be sent to the state president.[176] In the 1987 white election, the Conservative Party (CP) gained Overvaal within which Weiler's Farm falls and municipal elections pending in 1988 increase the pressure on the authorities to reduce the settlement's size by moving some residents. One consequence has been continuing allegations that squatters have been harassed by security forces and white residents. This pressure has weakened squatter unity, prompting divisions within the committee: some members have been accused of attending secret meetings with TPA officials.[177] While the threat of partial removal remains, so does the need for more effective organisation which alone could counter it.

Regardless of the outcome of negotiations at Weiler's Farm, the pressure facing official urbanisation policy will continue to give the authorities an interest in negotiating solutions to the squatter question. But they are likely to continue to seek to negotiate agreements which benefit some residents only and the extent to which bargaining yields gains for squatter communities will depend on their ability to build united organisation. By 1987, they had not yet achieved this.

TRADE UNIONS

Community groups pursued negotiation when they were forced to seek to organise, rather than simply mobilise, supporters. In some cases, the fact that some government decision-makers favoured negotiation with them[178] ensured that limited talks took place. But they did not develop into bargaining.

Housing bargaining has nevertheless occurred in the PWV; predictably, the parties have been trade unions and business. Unlike civic groups, unions have developed one of the preconditions for bargaining, an organised base on which negotiators rely for a mandate: they can bargain from a position of strength, not simply because other avenues have been cut off. They have also formed bargaining relationships with employers and some have sought to use these to negotiate housing issues.

Interests of unions and employers in housing issues

One of the country's largest unions, the National Union of Metal Workers (NUMSA), began to raise housing issues to defend the interests of its members. Workers who participated in company housing schemes could lose their homes when they were retrenched: in the metal industries alone, 100 000 jobs were lost between 1984 and 1987. Employer housing loans were redeemed over 25 years, but no worker could be sure of remaining continuously employed for that long and insurance companies refused to insure worker homeowners against loss of income through retrenchment.[179] A second motive, according to a NUMSA official, was a fear that home ownership would tie workers into financial commitments which would diminish their willingness to act collectively[180] — housing is thus also an organisational issue for the union.

Unions also see an interest in addressing the housing problems of the unemployed who, according to a spokesman for the Congress of South African Trade Unions (COSATU's) Springs branch , form a reserve army of labourers which could be used to undercut the power of the organised employed; unions could thus not fight for the interests of the employed only.[181] (Outside COSATU, an unemployed workers co-ordinating committee (UWCC), was, in 1987, investigating ways of addressing the housing needs of its constituency by organising the unemployed into building co-operatives.)[182] The COSATU official noted also that its alliance with the UDF and the adoption by some unions of the Freedom Charter compelled it to demand decent housing not only as a union issue but as a broader social goal.[183]

COSATU also sees the housing shortage as a consequence of government ideology, a view shared by officials of the National Council of Trade Unions (NACTU), who argued that the African housing shortage is caused by government attempts to restrict the number of Africans in the cities who are not migrant labourers.[184] A National Union of Metalworkers of South Africa (NUMSA) official adds that the lack of adequate housing is a way of controlling the movement of African workers and is part of a system of labour control which depresses wages in the interests of employers and the state.[185] This view has given unions an added incentive to use their bargaining power to support the housing demands of community groups: a key example is their attempt, in 1985 and 1986, to bargain a settlement of the Vaal rent boycott with local employers.

Employers' interest in negotiating over housing stems not only from their desire to maintain industrial peace by dealing with unions but from a recognition, particularly since the 1976 township based resistance, that better housing could help create a more productive and loyal workforce[186] as well as a 'more positive and stable climate within which to conduct business.'[187] Some employers have thus interacted not only with unions but with community groups and black local authorities in an attempt to seek housing solutions: one example is the east Rand industrialists' network (ERIN), a group of some forty, mainly American-owned, companies which tackles a variety of social issues, including housing, and which has attempted to resolve rent boycotts through negotiations with community leaders, the authorities and workers.[188] The townships where employers were most effectively involved in bargaining over housing, were, however, those in the Vaal triangle.

The catalyst to these negotiations was the Urban Foundation (UF), which had been formed by business leaders in response to the 1976 township conflict. Its aim was to improve the 'quality of life' in urban areas and, in particular, to encourage African home ownership. Its role as a lobby group and as a development agent in the townships — which enabled it to develop contacts with both the authorities and township communities — sometimes drew it into situations in which it had the opportunity to encourage negotiations between community groups and the authorities; one such opportunity arose during the Vaal rent boycott.[189]

Negotiations in the Vaal

The parties to the negotiations were the Vaal chamber of commerce and industries (VCCI), the Vaal trade union co-ordinating commitee (VTUCC), the Lekoa council (which administered the townships) and the Orange-Vaal development board (OVDB); all had an interest in negotiating a solution to the boycott. The VCCI feared its impact on the factory floor, union members were directly affected as township residents and the local authority's debt was worsening as the boycott continued. But it required a mediator, the UF, to bring them to the bargaining table.

In June 1985 the VTUCC met the VCCI; in July, a second meeting was attended also by council officials;[190] the meetings followed discussions, partly prompted by the UF, involving community groups and local officials as well as unions and employers.[191] This first attempt at negotiation ended on 24 July when, in reaction to the declaration of a state of emergency, the unions requested an indefinite postponement of the talks.[192] But pressure on all parties to negotiate persisted despite the emergency and in September, two detained community leaders, Rev Jeff Moselane and Mr Tom Manthata, asked the UF to attempt to re-open negotiations. Between November and January, four further meetings took place in an attempt to reconvene formal negotiations between the council and the VTUCC.[193]

Unlike the talks in other areas, those in the Vaal involved representatives of mass organisations, mandated by their members to pursue negotiations with *inter alia* the black local authority. But, like those elsewhere, they failed to achieve a settlement. A prime reason was the authorities' refusal to meet a key union demand — for an open air mass meeting with residents.[194] This was a necessary part of the bargaining process, since it would allow them to consult their constituents and seek a mandate from them: but, in December, the demand was rejected by the local National Party MP, Mr Chris Ballot, on 'security grounds' and this led to the dissolution of the talks. Mr Ballot had been acting as intermediary between the unions (and some community groups who later joined the talks) and the central authorities, who had a clear interest in the outcome; his decision could, therefore, have reflected the stance of central government.

The approach of Lekoa council representatives also contributed to the failure of the talks. At a meeting on 2 December, an employer proposal that an interim rent of R30 be paid, was agreed to by the unions but rejected by the council. On 12 December, R50 was proposed as an interim rent, to be paid until an RSC was established in the Vaal. The council rejected this too, suggesting instead a law to compel employers to deduct the full rent from workers' wage packets.[195] And, at the final meeting, in January, the unions accused the council of obstructing their attempts to obtain the use of a hall for a meeting. At this meeting, the talks were suspended, never to be resumed.[196]

These official responses appeared to reflect a broader attempt by state security planners to resist negotiations with unions and civic groups. Shortly before the agreement to resume talks, a document was submitted to the council entitled 'Strategy for the collection of arrear rental and service charges', which urged that 'no acknowledgement through negotiations must be given to revolutionary groups.'[197] It also directed that all action on rents be taken by mini-JMCs and suggested security measures for ending the boycott. Both the council's refusal to accept an interim settlement and Mr Ballot's refusal to allow the unions to meet residents were consistent with this approach; this suggests that, as in Tembisa, it was the local JMC, and the security strategy it represented, which obstructed negotiation.

33

Despite their failure, the Vaal talks were the most advanced negotiations over housing in the PWV area between 1983 and 1988; they bore all the characteristics of collective bargaining. Firstly, the antagonists had initially indicated a desire to achieve a settlement. Mr Louw, the town clerk of Lekoa, for instance, said on 5 July 1985 that the gesture of co-operation and goodwill from the VTUCC was encouraging and that the council was prepared to meet union and community representatives to sympathetically discuss their grievances.[198] Mr Petrus Tom of the VTUCC replied that it was pleased to learn that the council was prepared to meet civic groups.[199]

The VTUCC was also accountable to a sufficiently well organised constituency to represent a counterforce to the council and the state. The unions sought to further strengthen their base by involving the local branch of the Congress of South African Students (COSAS) and civic groups in the talks and discussing demands with them.[200] But their responsibility to their worker members remained a priority and, in November, a union meeting recommended that workers in the factories first be consulted before negotiations were resumed.[201] The unions' reliance on mandates from members also enabled them to talk to the councillors: the November meeting, despite calling for the resignation of councillors, mandated the VTUCC to meet any party which might facilitate a settlement of the boycott.[202] This opened the way to talks with councillors and enabled the unions to avoid the impasse on this issue which ended the Soweto talks.

During the months of negotiation which followed, the unions were able to introduce a new style of politics into the Vaal townships. The talks prompted meetings at which working class residents discussed the central issues affecting their lives in the townships; at the very least they educated themselves about the functioning and financing of the council, and the ways in which the townships were being administered. Negotiations had created space for organising, and the unions used it.

The fact that the antagonists repeatedly indicated a willingness to move from stated positions, and had come to recognise each other as *de facto* negotiating partners, fulfilled a third precondition for bargaining; only after several months did the council's refusal to cede on two issues prompt the collapse of talks. While they continued, neither side abandoned attempts to weaken the other: the boycott continued and, although the authorities did not evict rent defaulters while talks were in progress, after the declaration of the 1985 state of emergency, the state acted against community leaders — 7 966 people were detained, including members of the VTUCC[203] and, prior to the emergency, 22 Vaal civic leaders were already being held pending the outcome of a treason trial in which they were alleged to have conspired with the ANC to overthrow the state.[204] That bargaining continued in these circumstances testifies to the adversaries' interest in a settlement, despite their hostility to each other. That community groups believed they retained the strength to sustain bargaining in this climate was largely due to the organised strength of the unions, who were able to maintain their structures despite severe security action.

Since the end of the talks the eviction of tenants has resumed (as it did between the two sets of negotiations).[205] Yet by the end of 1987 the boycott continued, confirming that, despite sustained security action, the authorities retained a latent interest in negotiating a solution.

Housing bargaining elsewhere in the region

In the Vaal townships, business played a mediating role, and was an important catalyst to talks. But in other parts of the region, employers played a direct role in housing negotiations. In Springs during 1986 the FCI and the COSATU branch bargained over the financing of new housing in the nearby township of KwaThema[206] and in Brits, north of Pretoria, metal industry unionists negotiated with employers on the industries' pension fund board for money to purchase the township of Oukasie, which was threatened with removal.[207] These examples confirmed a growing union role in pressing, through negotiation, for improved housing; in several areas, they have been better able to pursue housing demands than community groups.

In Oukasie, most residents are organised workers who, in the absence of strong community organisations, turned to their unions to bargain on their behalf. On the east Rand, unions have withstood security action while community groups have not: nor is their involvement there in issues beyond the factories a new phenomenon. During the early-1980s the Germiston shop stewards' council played an important role in defending Katlehong squatters against action from the authorities.[208]

But there are limits to the unions' ability to play this role. Their power base lies in the factories rather than the townships — while they can threaten strike action to persuade employers to accept worker demands, they do not have the same leverage over township authorities. While they could help shape the development of organised mass civic associations, they could not assume their function. A NUMSA official notes that unions face conflicting demands when they tackle community issues. They are bound to act in the interests of their members, but their goals did not always coincide with those of the rest of the community; at times, the one might be achieved only at the expense of the other. Their role was thus to strengthen, not replace, community organisation and NUMSA was seeking a strategy which would address the whole range of demands for housing and amenities rather than demanding better housing only for its members.[209]

Unions are thus likely to remain a major force shaping township politics as well as talks over housing. Evidence of this was the emergence of housing demands on bargaining agendas in several industries and the steady development of housing bargaining in one of them.

35

Negotiating housing benefits in the metal industry

As noted above, unions and employers have a clear interest in negotiating housing issues: a recent survey of 350 companies employing more than one million employees, revealed that 63% provided housing aid to their staff.[210] These benefits have not been negotiated with unions but have been instituted unilaterally or in consultation with individual employees. On the mines, negotiations on the provision of family housing close to the workplace would offer unions a victory over a century of stringent controls on workers' freedom of movement and employers the prospect of a more stable workforce. During 1988 the NUM and De Beers Mines initiated a bargaining process over this issue. But during 1987 it was only in the metal industries, that housing bargaining became a growing aspect of union activity.

NUMSA has been involved in several instances of housing bargaining in the PWV. It has, for example, negotiated with a housing company, Lowcost Housing, and Union Steel (USCO) the terms of a scheme in which the employer agreed to subsidise worker housing provided by Lowcost: negotiations began because Lowcost wanted the union to encourage workers to participate. It has also negotiated with Highveld Steel over a company home ownership scheme for workers previously housed in hostels: the union argued that the company preferred a scheme in which workers would have to pay for housing to NUMSA's long-standing demand that it upgrade the hostels[211] but was nevertheless prepared to negotiate the terms of the scheme with the company.

Its most significant housing bargaining has, however, centred around its demand that money in the metal industry's pension fund be used for housing. The fund, to which unskilled and semi-skilled workers belong, was during the mid-1980s the fourth largest in the country, with assets worth approximately R1,6bn.[212] These talks are significant as the vast sums controlled by pension funds are seen as a key potential source of housing finance. Employers proposed the fund lend money to individual members, but union members of the fund board rejected this because the union did not want to place itself in the invidious position of having to evict its own members if they defaulted on repayments.[213] By the end of 1987 negotiations were still in process. Another approach to worker housing was suggested by bargaining in late 1987 and early 1988 with the Metal Box company over the use of its provident fund for housing. In terms of the company's proposed scheme, building societies would provide home loans while the fund members would cede to them worker contributions equalling 10% or 20% of the loan;[214] this would relieve NUMSA of the task of acting against its members. But the union fears that the scheme could threaten workers' collective strength by tying its members to commitments to financial institutions, reducing their solidarity with fellow workers. During 1988 the union had negotiated a research project to determine the demands of fund members.

Both these examples have prompted NUMSA to examine strategies for negotiating housing finance arrangements which will promote greater organised worker control over housing funds and delivery and which will not threaten worker unity. It hopes to develop proposals which will allow pension and provident fund money to be used to strengthen collective worker control over the funding, delivery and allocation of housing.

Housing bargaining: pattern of the future?

Unions' involvement in housing negotiation is unique because they have a well-organised constituency which can wield countervailing power to that of their bargaining partners. Their role will be limited because their base lies in the factories but, in Soweto, for example, the civic association has attempted to develop structures which could enable it also to bargain from an organised base. If community groups are to wield influence over decisions affecting their members, building this base will be their most important task; given their ability to remain organised under state of emergency conditions, unions could contribute to shaping the emergence of grassroots township organisation.

Through bargaining with employers, unions were also in 1987 beginning to seek influence over housing delivery. Because unions and employers, unlike community groups and the authorities, have developed a bargaining relationship, these negotiations were most likely to produce arrangements which would allow some township residents to win partial control over the planning, building and financing of their homes. If they do, these agreements will inevitably prompt negotiations with the authorities, who control the land on which housing must be developed. Union-employer bargaining is, therefore, the most likely immediate catalyst to housing negotiation between township residents and the authorities, directly or mediated by private developers.

CONCLUSION

The past three years have seen attempts by adversaries in the PWV, prompted by an impasse in which neither could entirely impose their will on the other, to negotiate housing issues. But the negotiations have not produced a settlement of the conflict and the impasse continues. This inquiry has attempted to pinpoint some of the potential for, and the obstacles to, negotiations which might break the present deadlock.

Despite the hostility of the adversaries to each other, it is significant that both central government reformists and community groups were on occasions willing to negotiate. Both were responding to a changed political situation in many townships, particularly in the eastern Cape.

Severe conflict, prompted originally by housing issues, had prevented official local authorities in several townships from carrying out administrative tasks which included housing allocation, provision of services and rent collection. Many communities were thus faced with some of the day-to-day problems of running their townships and housing themselves and some community groups attempted to respond by presenting alternative plans for township development and house construction,[215] of which a detailed plan developed in Langa was perhaps the clearest example. Their emergence offered state planners the prospect of resolving the housing question in ways which would enjoy community support and which might restore longer-term stability to these areas. In Langa, negotiations between local authorities and community and union groups prompted the establishment in 1986 of a special department of constitutional development and planning task force to investigate the feasibility of upgrading the township; the department was reported to have set aside R200m for upgrading Uitenhage and Port Elizabeth townships in negotiation with the eastern Cape branch of the UDF.

But this approach faced substantial opposition within the government.The Tembisa and Vaal cases provide evidence of the ability of security strategists to frustrate negotiation : the Langa negotiations met the same fate as did a similar exercise in the western Cape township of Zwelethemba, outside Worcester, where negotiations on upgrading, which involved a deputy cabinet minister and the police, as well as a private building society, were halted by the detention of community negotiators.

Nor was the government's security strategy the only obstacle to negotiation. Others included the reluctance of community groups to negotiate with, and the unwillingness of officials to bypass, the councillors; the absence of effective intermediaries who could have brought parties with an interest in negotiation to the bargaining table; the view of some activists that housing negotiation would obscure political objectives whose achievement could alone allow residents to meet their housing needs (although some who held this view were impelled to seek negotiation by organisational imperatives, they did not necessarily see it as a means of building long-term influence)[216]; and a similar view that local housing negotiation conflicted with the national strategies which anti-apartheid movements pursued.

But the last two views at least are giving way to a recognition that local negotiation over short-term demands may provide communities with the organisation they might need to pursue national objectives which traditional forms of mobilisation have failed to achieve. The reimposition of physical state control over the townships has prompted an increased awareness of the importance of grassroots organisation and of negotiation over short-term demands as a way of achieving it.

The need for organisation is particulary clear in informal settlements such as Weiler's Farm where the authorities face pressure from local whites to remove residents (as they did at Langa) and community unity is subject to severe stress. It was an internal schism in the Crossroads community, prompting an alliance between the authorities and leaders previously allied with the UDF, which triggered the mass relocation to Khayelitsha which other government strategies could not achieve. Divisions have usually been prompted by feuding over the distribution of scarce land and at Weiler's Farm they may emerge if the authorities try to move some residents while allowing others to remain. Doubts about the cohesion of squatter organisation are illustrated by the fears of some squatter leaders that the authorities could use a local authority to ensure that councillors obey the government rather than their constituents;[217] divisions can, of course, be countered only by effective organisation. But the growth of informal settlements presents the authorities with their most intractable problem and the stresses which it places on government urbanisation policy could allow squatter communities to make significant gains through negotiation if they are able to forge internal unity.

The most immediate source of housing negotiation, however, is likely to be bargaining between unions and employers; in this area, the influence of state security strategists is limited and bargaining relationships exist which are still to be created in the townships. In areas such as the Vaal, the unions have also sought to use their bargaining power and style to resolve township housing disputes, albeit with little success thus far.

Unions' entry into housing bargaining has raised possibilities for a new style of community organisation. Their stress on negotiating from a strength derived from grassroots structures in which negotiators are mandated by their constituents and their use of negotiation to strengthen organisation could offer community groups a model which would allow them to win power over township decisions.

Whether community groups' greater willingness to negotiate will be met by a similar response from the authorities depends on the outcome of divisions within the state between those who favour negotiation as a means to stability and those who advocate a combination of force and socio-economic upgrading. Thus far, the latter view has dominated. Prospects for negotiation will depend partly on the strengthening of the first view: a key test may be events in Soweto, where negotiation opportunities emerged most clearly, and a settlement there would have an impact elsewhere too.

But the outcome will depend partly on the ability of community groups to develop organised structures which would enable them to press for negotiation and make gains from it: in the PWV, these structures began to emerge only in Soweto. Only if they grow will community groups be able to make progress through bargaining. But negotiation might not have to await their emergence since community groups could use talks to demand the freedom to operate which might allow organisation to develop.

Even if these structures did emerge, however, bargaining might not develop unless mediators emerge who can bring the adversaries to the negotiating table. The housing shortage, and thus pressure for housing negotiating, will persist; but negotiation would be far more likely if mediation structures are created which would offer community groups and the authorities the possibility of negotiating the terms of the township development.

A starting point could be land availability agreements between the black local authorities and private developers created by regulations published in terms of the Black Communities Development Amendment Act.[218] These are contracts in which a black local authority allocates land to a developer, who must develop it in terms of conditions specified in the contract. Developers could thus negotiate the terms of development with community groups and then attempt to secure their acceptance by the local authority, in effect mediating between them. Any party with an interest in development could be a developer, including a utility company or provident fund; employers who negotiate housing agreements with unions could play this role and then appoint contractors to undertake the agreed development.

This highlights again unions' potential as a catalyst to housing negotiation; but in principle this model could also facilitate community involvement in housing delivery which could begin to make the exercise of grassroots community control over housing development a reality.

NOTES

1   Anstey M, Negotiation, mediation, arbitration in Barling J, Hillager C and Bluen S (eds) *Behaviour in organisations; SA Perspectives*, McGraw Hill, 1986, p851

2   SAIRR, *1984 Survey*, p375

3   De Vos T J, *Financing Low-Cost housing*, NBRI, paper presented at a seminar on finance for low-cost housing, August 1986, p3.

4   SAIRR, *1979 Survey*, p422, SAIRR, *1984 Survey*, p383; p385;p389; p395

5   Webb T, *Financing and Affordability*, case study analysis, Building Industries, Federation of South Africa (BIFSA) conference, Pretoria, 1983

6   Planact, *Langa: The case for upgrade*, Planact, Johannesburg, 1986

7   *The Star*, 2 June, 1984

8   *Sowetan*, 14 September, 1984

9   Daveyton city council correspondence, referring to SAIRR interview, on 21 September, 1987, pp4-5
The council claimed that the site-and-service charge remained R16,95, and that deposits for water and electricity remained R50. Reconnection fees had increased to R25, creche fees to R15 and burial fees and bioscope ticket to an undisclosed amount.

10 Interview 13, with an official of the Family Housing Association who lives in Daveyton, in Johannesburg on 23 March 1987, pp36-37; Interview 23, with a member of the then-defunct DAC, in Johannesburg on 17 June, 1987, pp22-23; Interview 30, with two officials of National Council of Trade Unions in Johannesburg on 15 July, 1987, pp13-14

11 Interview 30, pp11-12

12 Interview 39, with an official of ERAPO, in Johannesburg, on 19 August, 1987, pp15-16

13 Interview 39, p16

14 Daveyton city council correspondence, op cit, 21 September, 1987, p1

15 Daveyton city council correspondence, op cit, 21 September, 1987, p2

16 Interview 39; pp12-13 Daveyton city council correspondence, op cit, 21 September, 1987, p1

17 Interview 23, pp22-23

18 Interview 13

19 Interview 30, pp12-13

20 Interview 30, pp13-14

21 Interview 30, pp12-13

22 Alexander N, Aspects of Non-Collaboration in the Western Cape 1943-1963, in *Social Dynamics*, 12, 1, June 1986, pp1-14

23 ERAPO correspondence with SAIRR, referring to points requiring clarification, during October 1987, pp1-2

24 Interview 39, p5

25 Interview 11, with the assistant administration officer of the Daveyton council, in Daveyton on 18 March, 1987, pp30-33

26 Interview 39, pp16-18

27 ERAPO correspondence op cit, October 1987, p3

28 SAIRR, *1983 Survey*, p258

29 Interview 23, pp22-23

30 Interview 34, with a reporter of the *Sowetan*, in Industria West, on 31 July, 1987, p2

31 Interview 30, p9; p23

32 Interview 23, pp26-27

33 Interview 30, pp11-12; Interview 34, p2; Interview 39, pp13-14 Daveyton city council correspondence, op cit, 21 September 1987, p2

34 Interview 39, pp12-13

35 ERAPO correspondence, op cit, October 1987, p2

36   Interview 11, p27
37   Interview with town secretary of Tokoza, in Tokoza, on 11 August 1987, pp7-8
38   Interview 30, p16; Interview 23, p33
39   Interview 39, p9
40   Residence (sic), Asinamali Ya Renti (pamphlet), undated
41   Interview 12, with a lawyer, in Johannesburg, on 8 July, 1987
42   Interview 28, p1; p2; p4; pp6-7
43   *New Nation*, 3-16 July, 1986
44   *The Star*, 15 July, 1986
45   *The Star*, 30 April, 1987
46   Interview 28, p12-13
47   Interview 28, p7
      Presumably the council could still issue eviction notices, the decision for
      which had been taken before its dissolution. Otherwise the evictions would
      have been *ultra vires*.
48   *The Star*, 1 August 1986
49   *The Star*, 1 September 1986
50   *Sowetan*, 19 September, 1986; Interview 35, with an African ex-administrator of
      the Tembisa city Council in Johannesburg, on 6 August 1987, p10
51   Interview 35, p10
52   Interview 35, pp5-6
53   *Natal Witness*, 1 November, 1986
54   Interview 28, pp19-20
55   Interview 35, p12
56   *Natal Witness*, 1 November 1986
57   Department of community development, *Guidelines for self-building for local
      authorities and utility companies using national housing funds*, November 1983
58   *Beeld*, 24 June 1986
59   Black Communities Development Amendment Act (no 74) of 1986
      See also the following regulations published in terms of the principal act:
      Government Notice R1897, Government Gazette 10431 (Regulation
      Gazette 3998), 'Regulations relating to township establishment and land
      use,' 12 September, 1986; Government Notice R1899, Government
      Gazette 10432. (Regulation Gazette 3998), 'Regulations relating to the
      determination of the price of public land,' on 12 September, 1986;
      Government Notice R1098, Government Gazette 10431 (Regulation
      Gazette 3998), Amendment of Leasehold Regulations, 1985, 12 September
      1986.
60   Interview 35, p14
61   Interview 1, with the deputy town clerk of the Tembisa city council, in Tembisa,
      on 6 March, 1987, p6
62   Interview 6, with an official of Bilhard Construction, in Kempton Park, on 11
      March, 1987, p4
63   *The Star*, 28 July, 1986
64   *The Star*, 15 July, 1986
65   Interview 46, with the town clerk of the Tembisa city council in Tembisa, on 15
      September 1987, pp39-40
66   Interview 46, p39
67   Interview 46, p41
68   *Weekly Mail*, 1 August, 1986
69   Ibid
70   Interview 28, p3; p7
71   Interview 28, p8; Interview 46, p3; p4; p41
      The town clerk of Tembisa said that he was unaware that the TCA's lawyers
      had had any contact with the legal representatives of the Tembisa local
      authority, and that neither he nor the local authority had received demands
      referred to in the text. The town clerk's evidence however is contradicted

by correspondence from the legal representatives of the Tembisa local authority to the TCA's lawyers. This correspondence cannot be produced as evidence because such action would constitute a breach of professional etiquette on the part of the TCA's legal representatives.

72   *New Nation*, 31 July 1986
73   *Sowetan*, 26 September 1986
74   Interview 46, p32
75   Interview 46, p38; Interview 28, pp17-18
76   Interview 28, pp17-18
77   Interview 36, pp16-18
78   Bekker S and Humphries R, *From control to confusion - The changing role of administration boards in South Africa*: 1971-1983, Shuter and Shooter, Pietermaritzburg, 1985, p100
79   Hendler P, Capital accumulation, the State and the Housing Question, unpublished MA dissertation, university of the Witwatersrand, Johannesburg, 1986, p103
80   Interview 49, with a PFP, MP in Cape Town, on 2 October 1987
81   Interview 28, pp13-15
82   Interview 28, pp15-17
83   *Citizen*, 29 August, 1986; *The Star*, 7 September, 1986; *Sowetan*, 12 December, 1987; *Sowetan*, 20 March, 1987; *The Star*, 3 April, 1987; *New Nation*, 7 May, 1987
84   Interview 25, with the town clerk of the Soweto city council, in Soweto, on 30 June and 2 July, 1987, pp40-41
85   Interview 25, p28
86   Interview 25, pp30-31
87   Interview 25, pp42-44
88   Interview 25, pp2-3
89   Interview 25, p15
90   Interview 25, p2
91   Interview 25, p33-39
92   *Sowetan*, 27 May, 1987
93   *The Star*, 3 July, 1987; *Weekly Mail*, 17 July 1987
94   Interview 25, pp40-41
95   *Sowetan*, 20 May 1987
96   Interview 37, with two officials of AZAPO, in Johannesburg on 7 August and 10 August, 1987, pp16-17
97   *Sowetan*, 20 May, 1987; Moleke B, Points from meeting with Soweto town clerk, on 18 November 1986, 26 November, 1986, and February 1987
98   Moleke B, Points from meeting with Soweto town clerk, on 12 February 1987
99   *The Star*, 23 April, 1987
100   *Sowetan*, 4 August, 1987
101   Advice centres association, ACA News, Vol 1, no 1, September 1987, p1
102   Interview 37, pp18-19
103   Interview 18, with a member of ACA in Johannesburg on 18 May 1987, p3
104   Interview 18, p39; pp49-51; pp51-52
105   Interview 40, with an official of the AIM, WFC and the WNH, at Wilgespruit on 21 August 1987, pp 19-22
106   Interview 40, p25; pp20-21; p23
107   Interview 37 pp19-21
108   Interview 40, pp20-21; p23
109   Interview 40, pp39-40; Interview 25, pp18-23
110   Interview 44, with an official of the SCA, in Braamfontein, on 8 September 1987, pp40-41
111   Interview 45, pp40-41
112   Interview 45, pp42-43
113   Interview 45, pp43-45
114   Interview 45, pp55-57

115 Interview 45, pp46-48
116 *The Star*, 29 April, 1987
117 Moleke B, Memorandum to Soweto town clerk, on 4 December 1986
118 Interview 37, pp14-15
119 Interview 37, pp40-41
120 Interview 45, pp39-40; *The Star*, 5 August, 1987; *The Star*, 7 August, 1987
121 Moleke B, op cit, 18 November 1986, p3
122 Moleke B, op cit, 26 November 1986, p2
123 Moleke B, op cit, 3 February 1987, p1
124 Moleke B, op cit, 12 February 1987, p1
125 Interview 25, pp13-14
126 Interview 25, pp47-49
127 Interview 25
128 Interview 45, pp20-23
129 Interview 18, pp15-17
130 *The Star*, 7 August, 1987
131 Moleke B, op cit, 26 November 1986, p2
132 Wilkinson P, *A place to live: the resolution of the African housing crisis in* *Johannesburg 1944 to 1954*, African Studies Seminar, university of the Witwatersrand, July 1981, p23
133 Department of constitutional development and Planning, *White Paper on Urbanisation*, Pretoria, 1986, p71
134 The term refers to new areas which have been approved for the establishment of factories and industries, outside the boundaries of the major metropolitan areas.
135 SAIRR, *1986 Survey*, p43
136 SAIRR, *1986 Survey*, pp42-43
137 This represented a significant change in state policy. The last policy statement on the issue had been during 1983 (see: Department of community development, op cit, November, 1983, p4)

   Controlled squatting was defined as squatting which had been planned by a qualified official body, and over which a certain amount of control was exercised; or which started off as uncontrolled squatting and was later controlled. In such a situation squatters would be permitted to erect their structures in an identified area which had, to a certain extent, been orderly planned. Rudimentary services would be provided, control would be exercised over the number of squatters, and they could be charged for the use of services.

138 Interview 10, with an official of the department of development planning, in Pretoria, on 16 March, 1987, pp59-60
139 Interview 10, pp59-60; Cole J, *Crossroads - The Politics of Reform and Repression 1977-1986*, Ravan Press, Johannesburg, 1987, pp117-164
140 Mashego M, '*Caught in the web of orderly urbanisation - forced removals in Langa*, Planact, Johannesburg, 1986
141 *The Star* 8 Spetember, 1987
142 Interview 41, with two officials of the Walkerville Light for the Homeless (WLH) and the Weilers Farm Squatters Committee in Johannesburg, on 31 August 1987, pp60-67
143 Interview 41, pp60-67
144 SAIRR, *1983 Survey*, p275
145 *Sowetan*, 31 March, 1987
146 *Business Day*, 4 August, 1987
147 *New Nation*, 17 July, 1987; *Sunday Times*, 24 May, 1987; *Sowetan*, 12 August, 1987; *The Star*, 23 July, 1987
148 Interview 41; *Sowetan*, 24 February, 1987; *The Star*, 8 July, 1987; *Business Day*, 16 April, 1987
149 *The Star* 8 July, 1987
150 Interview 41; *The Star*, 8 July, 1987;

151 Department of constitutional development and planning, *Greater Pretoria Guide Plan 1984*, Government printer, Pretoria, p54

152 Department of constitutional development and planning *Draft Guide Plan for the East Rand/Far East Rand*, 1984, Pretoria, p214

153 Department of constitutional development and planning, *Central Witwatersrand Draft Guide Plan*, Pretoria, 1986, pp150-152

154 Department of constitutional development and planning, *Vaal River complex Guide Plan* 1982, p78

155 *Sowetan*, 21 November, 1986

156 *The Star*, 21 July, 1987; *Business Day*, 16 April, 1987; *Sowetan*, 20 May, 1987; *Sowetan*, 8 September, 1987

157 Interview 41, p56 *The Star*, 14 September, 1987

158 Interview 41, p59

159 *Sowetan*, 27 November 1986; *The Star*, 28 November 1986; *Sowetan*, 7 January, 1987; *Business Day*, 7 January, 1987; *The Star*, 26 March, 1987; *The Star*, 15 July, 1987; *Business Day*, 14 July, 1987

160 *New Nation*, 19-25 March, 1987

161 Interview 41, p41

162 *Sunday Times*, 11 January 1987

163 *Sowetan*, 24 November 1986

164 *The Star*, 3 April, 1987

165 *The Star*, 28 August, 1986

166 *Sunday Times*, 11 January, 1987

167 *The Star*, 3 April, 1987

168 Interview 25, pp54-55

169 Interview 41, pp50-51; p55

170 Interview 41, pp22-23

171 Interview 41, pp17-20

172 Interview 41, p53; p46

173 Interview 41, pp47-48

174 Interview 41, pp41-45

175 Interview 41, p40

176 *The Star*, 29 January, 5 March and 13 March 1987

177 Interview 41

178 Interview 48, with four senior officials of the department of development planning, in Cape Town, on 2 October, 1987

179 Interview 44, with an official of NUMSA in Braamfontein, on 7 September 1987, p2

180 Interview 44, p5

181 Interview 42, with three officials of the Springs local branch of COSATU, in Springs, on 1 September, 1987, pp18-19

182 Interview 14, with a person participating in an unemployed workers projects, in Braamfontein, on 3 March, 1987

183 Interview 42, p18-19

184 Interview 30, pp1-2

185 Interview 44, pp41-43

186 Leach J, *Employer Black Housing Experiences*, in International Compensation (Pty) Limited (eds), *Black Housing in 1987*, Proceedings of a symposium, 1987, pp 43-44

187 Leach J, op cit, 1987, p43

188 Leach J, op cit, 1987, p46

189 Interview 8, with two officials of the UF in Johannesburg, on 12 March 1987, pp13-14

190 Untitled, minutes of meeting between VCCI and VTUCC, in Vereeniging, in the board room of the SA Permanent Building Society, on 13 June 1985; and 5 July 1985

191 See for instance: Lekoa city council correspondence to the chairman of the

Bophelong delegation, on 28 February, 1985; Untitled, minutes of meeting between members of the Vaal FOSATU shop stewards council, in Vereeniging, on 11 May 1985; FOSATU Vaal shop stewards council correspondence to COSAS and civic organisations, on 13 May, 1985; Untitled, minutes of meeting between FOSATU Vaal local branch, industrial aid society, MAWU, sweet food and allied workers union, COSAS, CCAWUSA, OVGWU, and Sharpville civic association, on 16 May 1985, in Vereeniging; Untitled, minutes of meeting between MAWU, FAWUSA, OVGWU, CUSA, CCAWUSA as well as other trade unions and civic organisations, on 31 May 1985, in Vereeniging; VCCI correspondence to FOSATU, on 5 June 1985

192   Untitled, minutes of meeting between various trade unions, on 24 July 1985, in the SA Perm building, in Vereeniging.

193   See for instance: Lekoa city council correspondence to the Boipatong civic association, 31 October 1985; Untitled, minutes of meeting between shop stewards and members of various trade unions, on 2 November 1985, at Mphatlathsanehall; Lekoa city council correspondence to the VTUCC, 19 November 1985; Untitled, minutes of meetings between the VTUCC, the VCCI, the Lekoa city council and other community organisations, on 22 November, 2 and 12 December 1985 and 17 January, 1986, in the Riviera hotel, Vereeniging;

194   Minutes of meeting, op cit, on 22 November, 1985

195   Minutes of meeting, op cit, on 12 December 1985

196   Minutes of meeting, op cit, on 17 January 1986

197   *Weekly Mail*, 1 August, 1986

198   Minutes of meeting, op cit, on 5 July 1985, p4; p6

199   Ibid

200   Minutes of meeting, op cit, 11 and 16 May 1985

201   Minutes of meeting, op cit, on 2 November 1985

202   Ibid

203   SAIRR, *1986 Survey*, p455

204   SAIRR, *1986 Survey*, p513

205   *The Star*, 11 August 1986, reported 10 families evicted in Bophelong; *The Star*, 13 August 1986, and *The Star* 13 August 1986, reported a total of 5 families evicted in Sharpeville; *Sowetan*, 13 August 1986, reported 15 families evicted in Zamdela and Sebokeng; *Sowetan,* 10 September 1986, reported 10 families evicted in Boipatong; *Sowetan*, 28 January 1987, and 22 June 1987, as well as *The Star*, 19 June 1987, reported a total of 38 families evicted in Vaal townships; *The Star*, 20 March 1987, reported a further five families evicted in Sharpeville

206   Interview 42, p8; Interview 44, p10

207   Interview 44, p11

208   Interview 42, pp57-58

209   Interview 44, pp14-15; pp18-19

210   Dickens D, *Employer reaction to Black Housing*, in International Compensation (Pty) Limited, *Black Housing in 1987*, op cit, 1987, p1

211   Interview 44, pp13-14; p31

212   Interview 44, pp32-33

213   Interview 44, p36; p51; p54

214   Interview 44; Annexure G (Untitled), Metal Industries Approach for expanding Homeownership among Lower-income employees, 28 April, 1987

215   Planact, op cit, *Weekly Mail* 8-14 November, 1985

216   Interview 37, p1; p31; pp20-21

217   Interview 41, p55; pp73-74

218   Refer to footnote 59; Interview 50, with official of the UF, in Cape Town, on 5 October, 1987, pp2-10

The South African Institute of Race Relations is a non-profitmaking organisation seeking to foster non-violent processes of change towards democracy in South Africa. It has no party political affiliations. Membership is open to all, irrespective of race, colour, creed, nationality, or country of residence

If you would like to join the Institute and/or receive regular copies of the annual *Survey* and our other publications (including back copies of the *Survey*), please write to the Membership Manager, SAIRR, P O Box 31044, Braamfontein, 2017 South Africa.